T0114481

EXPERIENCING
the
RESURRECTION

EXPERIENCING
the
RESURRECTION

The Everyday Encounter That Changes Your Life

HENRY & MELVIN
BLACKABY

MULTNOMAH

EXPERIENCING THE RESURRECTION

Scripture quotations are taken from the New King James Version®. Copyright © 1982 by Thomas Nelson Inc. Used by permission. All rights reserved.

Italics in Scripture quotations indicate the authors' added emphasis.

Trade Paperback ISBN 978-0-525-65431-5
Hardcover ISBN 978-1-59052-757-3
eBook ISBN 978-0-307-56154-1

Published in the United States by Multnomah, an imprint of the Crown Publishing Group, a division of Penguin Random House LLC, New York.

MULTNOMAH® and its mountain colophon are registered trademarks of Penguin Random House LLC.

The Library of Congress has cataloged the hardcover edition as follows:
Blackaby, Henry T., 1935–
    Experiencing the Resurrection : the everyday encounter that changes your life / Henry Blackaby, Melvin Blackaby. — 1st ed.
        p. cm.
    ISBN 978-1-59052-757-3
    1. Jesus Christ—Resurrection. 2. Christian life. I. Blackaby, Melvin D. II. Title.
    BT482.B43 2008
    232'.5—dc22

                              2007033766

CONTENTS

INTRODUCTION—The Validation 1

PART ONE

THE RESURRECTION IN THE HEART AND MIND OF GOD

CHAPTER 1—The Reality of Sin: We Perish 11

CHAPTER 2—The Father's Eternal Purpose 25

PART TWO

THE RESURRECTION IN THE LIFE OF THE LORD JESUS

CHAPTER 3—The Reality of Sin: He Died 41

CHAPTER 4—The Reality of Salvation: He Rose 59

CHAPTER 5—The Reality of Eternity: He Is Alive 74

PART THREE
The Resurrection in the Believer's Experience

CHAPTER 6—Resurrection Life 89

CHAPTER 7—Resurrection and the Uncommon Life 107

CHAPTER 8—Resurrection Peace 120

CHAPTER 9—Resurrection Joy 133

CHAPTER 10—Resurrection Power 147

CHAPTER 11—Resurrection Authority 162

CHAPTER 12—Resurrection Confidence 177

CHAPTER 13—Resurrection Hope 192

CONCLUSION—Never the Same Again 207

THE VALIDATION

That I may know Him and the power of His
resurrection...
—PHILIPPIANS 3:10

There is power in the gospel to set people completely free from the destructive power of sin and to fill their lives with all the fullness of God. That gospel includes the cross, the resurrection, and the sending of the Holy Spirit at Pentecost. All three are equally important for the believer to understand and experience.

This book will focus on the power of the resurrection as the necessary completion of the work accomplished on the cross. As much as the cross has been a central theme for believers throughout the ages, without the resurrection, the cross is meaningless.

If there were only the cross, sin would win—as the apostle Paul made clear:

If Christ is not risen, your faith is futile; you are still in your sins! Then also those who have fallen asleep in Christ have perished. If in this life only we have hope in Christ, we are of all men the most pitiable. (1 Corinthians 15:17–19)

The resurrection is proof of Christ's victory over sin and our hope of salvation.

The resurrection, however, is not a doctrine to be pondered but an invitation to experience the living Christ in your life. And

If there were only the cross, sin wins.

that's the reason for this book. If you don't appropriate all that God has provided through the resurrection, it's of no value to your life. We want you to do more than gain knowledge of the resurrection; we want you to *experience* the resurrection in your daily walk with the risen Christ. For the resurrection is not just an event that occurred in the first century. It continues to impact lives to this day. In reality, not only was Christ resurrected—you too are raised to new life when you're in Him. This is the gift of God to all who put their faith in His Son.

In Paul's words about his relationship to Jesus Christ, he said he wanted to "know Him and the power of His resurrection" (Philippians 3:10). This word *know* is more than head knowledge. It's experiential, and it touches every part of your life.

If you watch the life of the average Christian, you'll see little or no evidence of this incredible resurrection power that raised Christ from the dead. But this is exactly the power that's available to all who have accepted the risen Christ into their lives as their Lord and Savior.

Consider the encouragement about this resurrection power that Paul gave to the church in Ephesus as he offered his prayer for them:

> …that the God of our Lord Jesus Christ, the Father of glory, may give to you the spirit of wisdom and revelation in the knowledge of Him, the eyes of your understanding being enlightened; that you may know what is the hope of His calling, what are the riches of the glory of His inheritance in the saints, and what is the exceeding greatness of *His power toward us who believe,* according to the working of *His mighty power which He worked in Christ when He raised Him from the dead* and seated Him at His right hand in the heavenly places, far above all principality and power and might and dominion, and every name that is named, not only in this age but also in that which is to come. And He put all things under His feet, and gave Him to be head over all things to the church, which is His body, the fullness of Him who fills all in all. (Ephesians 1:17–23)

The resurrection power that raised Christ from the dead, then seated Him at the right hand of the Father and put Him over all principalities and powers, is the same power given to us. Should that make a difference in our lives? Should we be afraid of spiritual warfare? Is there anything we cannot overcome if we're walking with Christ?

Listen carefully: the battle is won! Don't believe Satan's lie that we have to do battle with him. Simply tell him, "You've already been defeated! And the same power that defeated you is the same power that now resides in my life." Don't get caught up in the fad of spiritual warfare that keeps you so busy fighting Satan that you have no time to follow Christ. The war's over! This is the practical expression of the resurrection, and it's available to you.

When you become a Christian, you're set in a wholly different dimension in which you can see what others don't see. As Jesus told His disciples, "It has been given to you to know the mysteries of the kingdom of heaven, but to them it has not been given" (Matthew 13:11). If you've been given ability to understand the mysteries of God, are you using your spiritual senses to detect the activity of God? Or do you act like the world, ignoring God until you need Him to bail you out of a crisis? You need to know what God is doing and then make whatever adjustment is needed to participate in His redemptive activity.

As a Christian, you're to be a witness for Christ—a visible demonstration of every truth God has said. But the religious culture in which we live encourages us just to practice religious activity. As a result, we misunderstand our relationship with God and miss out on experiencing His power. Unfortunately, many Christians are living way below their potential, believing they'll never be anything but ordinary. But, as Christians, we're children of God! If we're faithful in a little, He can make us rulers over much.

You've been given the opportunity to function in the realm of resurrection power—the most exciting life you could ever imagine. What then could God do in your life if He knew you were wholly yielded to Him? What could He do in you and through you if you believed He has *already* blessed you with every

You've been given the opportunity to function in the realm of resurrection power--the most exciting life imaginable.

spiritual blessing, delivered you out of the kingdom of darkness, and taken you who were dead in sin and made you fully alive in Christ?

Are you willing to let Him use you?

Or are you settling for the ordinary—satisfied with being insignificant?

THE LIVING WORD

As we consider the event of the resurrection and its present impact upon our lives, we'll stay close to the Scriptures. They'll be our guide to a deeper understanding of what God has done on our behalf. They contain an accurate account of the resurrection event and its timeless application to believers today. As you seek to experience the power of the resurrection in your life, you can anticipate the living Word of God revealing to you the riches of God's provision.

All you need to know about the resurrection is found in the Scriptures, and the Holy Spirit will apply them directly to your life. The key is not to "discover" truth, but to come with an open heart, into which the Holy Spirit will *reveal* truth. And that truth will set you free.

Remember, studying the resurrection is not an academic exercise. Our focus is not merely information, but application. True faith is based not upon knowing about Christ, but upon experiencing Him in our daily lives. A dry, scholastic, impersonal knowledge of God does not bring life. True knowledge of God is always *personal, powerful,* and *life changing.* If you aren't willing to allow Christ to make significant changes in your life, this book is not for you.

The first step in this journey is knowledge. You must *know* the truth and understand what God has done in the resurrection.

Second, you must *believe* it's true for *your* life. The Holy Spirit has been assigned to help you accept the truth as real, by testifying to your spirit that what you're seeing is true.

Third, you must *receive* the truth into your life. It isn't good enough to know the truth or even believe the truth. You must *embrace it as yours.*

Last, you must *live* the truth. That means taking what you've learned and *acting* upon it—making it a part of your daily life.

Move through this entire process, and you'll find new life in Christ—a life beyond anything you could imagine.

Abraham was someone who went through this process of living out his faith. "He did not waver at the promise of God through unbelief, but was strengthened in faith, giving glory to God, and being fully convinced that what He had promised He was also able to perform. And therefore '*it was accounted to him for righteousness*'" (Romans 4:20–22). Like Abraham, when you hear the truth of God in His Word, believe it with all your heart and hold on to it. Ask Him to implement it in your life. Have the determination of Paul, whose life goal included this: "that I may know Him and the power of His resurrection, and the fellowship of His sufferings, being conformed to His death, if, by any means, I may attain to the resurrection from the dead" (Philippians 3:10–11).

So many Christians are missing out on abundant life in Christ because they haven't understood how the resurrection completes the cross. The resurrection is the key that unlocks the door, the validation code giving us access to what Christ accomplished on the cross. And it will profoundly transform your life.

So get ready for new life in Christ.

The Resurrection in the Heart and Mind of God

THE REALITY OF SIN: WE PERISH

*For God so loved the world that He gave His only
begotten Son, that whoever believes in Him should
not perish but have everlasting life.*
—JOHN 3:16

The wonderful truth of God is a reality impossible for the
average person to grasp.

This dilemma is primarily because God is holy and moves on
a moral plane infinitely higher than that of sinful humanity. His
nature is wrapped up in perfect love. His thoughts are pure. His
ways are righteous. God exists in a place where our imagination
has never been.

Fortunately, however, God reveals Himself to us so we can know His thoughts and His ways. He says, "Call to Me, and I will answer you, and show you great and mighty things, which you do not know" (Jeremiah 33:3). When it comes to the resurrection, that's how we must go about learning. It's crucial that we understand *God's* perspective and not try to impose our thoughts upon Him.

Our need for the resurrection is brought home to us through the conviction of our spiritual deadness.

The clearest difference between God and His creation is found in salvation. He is holy; we are sinful. He is all-powerful; we are completely helpless. He is all-knowing; we are ignorant of spiritual things. He is self-existent; we are totally dependent upon His mercy and grace.

The gospel implies our great need. From God's perspective, we perish apart from all that He has done for us:

The cross was necessary because of the work of sin in our lives.

The resurrection was necessary because the cross put Christ to death on our behalf.

Pentecost was necessary to implement the new life that came as a result of the resurrection.

Our need for these acts of God through the gospel is brought home to us through the reality of our guilty conscience and the conviction of our spiritual deadness.

A GUILTY CONSCIENCE

It's hard to keep up with the fast pace of changing technology. As soon as you purchase "the latest thing," it's already out of date. But when something totally new hits the market, it seems to be the envy of everyone.

When cell phones first were invented and available for public use, few people had them. There was one lady, however, who had a cell phone and was very proud of it. One day she left it on a table at a busy restaurant and walked out. She quickly ran back into the establishment. Four businessmen were already seated at the table where she'd been. She asked if they'd seen it, but they all said no.

The restaurant manager, however, had an idea. He led the woman behind the counter and let her use the restaurant's phone to dial her cell phone number. Immediately they heard the ring and followed the sound back to her original table. It was emanating from a leather briefcase belonging to the man who was the first to arrive at the table for lunch.

The man began to sweat. His face turned red. He was caught!

This man, like all of us, had a moral conscience that told him it was wrong to steal the phone, but he chose to ignore his instincts. That's our problem. We ignore that which we innately know to be true and are swayed by a corrupt nature that's utterly self-centered. That sinful nature is a cruel master that always leads to ultimate destruction of the human soul.

SPIRITUAL BEINGS

All people instinctively know there's a God, whether or not they choose to respond to Him.

God made us in His own image. That is, we were created as spiritual beings with the capacity to know God and respond to Him as He reveals Himself to us. But the relationship for which we were created has been derailed by sin. The damaging effect of sin has been inflicted upon every human being who has ever come upon the earth.

God's Word declares that "all have sinned and fall short of the glory of God" (Romans 3:23). Nobody has escaped the influence and effect of sin—and that effect is fatal. Not only has it separated you from a relationship with God, but it keeps you from restoring that relationship on your own.

Paul's words in Romans 3 describe what sin does:

1. It makes you unrighteous and separates you from God.
2. It keeps you from understanding God.
3. It keeps you from seeking God.
4. It causes you to turn to other things, leaving you worthless, setting you on the road to depravity.

5. It ultimately causes you to lose the fear of God. And when you lose that, there's no deterrent to the destructive powers of sin. You can't stop your downward plunge away from God.

There's no way to keep yourself from these consequences of sin and eternal separation from a holy God. So is there any hope?

Absolutely! But only because there's a merciful God who loves us.

Read over the following passage from Romans 1:16–25, 28 as we consider the human condition and a merciful God who desires to save us from sin. Paul here describes the

When you lose the fear of God, you can't stop your downward plunge away from God.

tragic predicament of every human being and our need for God's intervention:

For I am not ashamed of the gospel of Christ, for it is the power of God to salvation for everyone who believes, for the Jew first and also for the Greek. For in it the right-eousness of God is revealed from faith to faith; as it is written, "The just shall live by faith." For the wrath of God is revealed from heaven against all ungodliness and unrighteousness of men, who suppress the truth in un-righteousness, because what may be known of God is manifest in them, for God has shown it to them. For since the creation of the world His invisible attributes are clearly seen, being understood by the things that are made, even His eternal power and Godhead, so that they are without excuse, because, although they knew God, they did not glorify Him as God, nor were thankful, but became futile in their thoughts, and their foolish hearts were darkened. Professing to be wise, they became fools, and changed the glory of the incorruptible God into an image made like corruptible man—and birds and four-footed animals and creeping things. Therefore God also gave them up to uncleanness, in the lusts of their hearts, to dishonor their bodies among themselves, who exchanged the truth of God for the lie, and worshiped and served the creature rather than the Creator, who is blessed forever. Amen.… And even as they did not like to retain God in their knowledge, God gave them over to a debased mind, to do those things which are not fitting.

This is a profound passage that we aren't able to fully dissect in this book, but we want to impress upon you its basic intent. Let's summarize what Paul is saying with two statements.

First, by *accepting* the revelation of God, you are brought into a relationship with Him that produces blessings in your life.

Though you're a sinner, God imparts His righteousness upon you as you put your faith in Christ and turn from your sin.

Second, by *rejecting* this revelation of God, you are kept from a relationship with Him and are brought under the bondage of your own ignorance. God gives you freedom to choose your own course of action, but you remain a sinner under the wrath of God.

To accept or reject God is your choice—but you'll be held accountable for your actions. You're absolutely free to determine the direction of your life, but you're not free to determine the consequences of the choices you make.

GOD SPEAKS

God reveals Himself to all mankind in two ways: through *the gospel* and through *His wrath.* The former delivers the repentant one *from* sin, and the latter delivers the unrepentant one *to* sin.

Both revelations are parallel and continuous. That is, *God's righteousness* is being revealed at all times through the preaching

Sometimes we aren't ready to respond to the gospel until we go through the wrath of God.

of the gospel of salvation. But also, *God's wrath* is always being revealed through His abandonment of humans to the consequences of their sinful choices.

The presence of evil and sin alerts people to the presence of God and His mercy. God's mercy, however, is at work in both His righteousness and His wrath. For both prompt men and women to repent and turn to God. Sometimes we aren't ready to respond to God's revelation in the gospel until we go through the wrath of God and recognize our need for salvation.

Let's look more closely at a few verses within the Romans 1 passage quoted above. Paul says in verses 16–17 that the gospel has the power for salvation that makes one righteous before God. In a right relationship with God, the believer can experience the joy of life as He intended. Through faith we receive the gift of salvation and begin to walk in an intimate love relationship with the God of the universe.

The gospel of Jesus Christ is God's clearest revelation of Himself. The incarnation, the crucifixion, the resurrection, and the sending of His Spirit together represent mankind's only hope.

Although God has revealed Himself in many ways, Jesus Christ is the climax of that revelation. When you receive Jesus into your life, you receive all the blessings of God. He's the answer to the question, "Who is God and how can I know Him?" Scripture says, "There is one God and one Mediator between God and men, the Man Christ Jesus, who gave Himself a ransom for all" (1 Timothy 2:5–6). Through Christ, we can be in right standing with a holy God.

Paul, however, also says that the rejection of God's revelation leaves you unrighteous and destined for utter ruin. Romans 1:18–32 describes what it looks like to turn away from God and live a self-centered life. Because we were created in the image of God, we have the capacity to recognize Him and therefore respond to Him. In every step that people take toward Him, He gives them opportunity to know more. For as verse 19 says, "What may be known of God is manifest in them, for God has shown it to them."

SIXTH SENSE

We each have a soul. We each have a spirit that can perceive God.

Don't stop with your five senses—move to the sixth sense. We see, hear, smell, touch, and taste so that we can experience the physical world around us. But we also have a spirit that allows us to experience the spiritual world in which we live. *You are a spiritual being.* It isn't just that we "know" deep down there must be a God, but that God Himself is causing us to sense His presence deep within. He responds to our sincere seeking and our longing to know our Creator.

Jesus said that He would send the Holy Spirit to testify to our spirits that we might know Him: "When the Helper comes, whom I shall send to you from the Father, the Spirit of truth who proceeds from the Father, He will testify of Me" (John 15:26).

Our world is so sophisticated in technology and the complexities of scientific discovery, yet many are content to live in a self-imposed ignorance in the area of the spiritual. They feel very comfortable to express ignorance of spiritual things and to be indifferent and complacent. They say, "Nobody can know God, so why waste time seeking Him?"

Paul utterly opposed this attitude. He said in verse 18 of Romans 1 that man is ignorant of the truth not because this truth is difficult to learn but because man has "suppress[ed] the truth" that is uncomfortably clear.

Our biggest problem is that we're afraid to give God control of our lives.

Man's problem is an ungodly *response* to the truth. The biggest problem for human beings is that they're afraid to give God control of their lives. They're content with a self-centered existence, for sin feeds their selfish desires.

THE CHALLENGE OF TRUTH

The Polish astronomer Copernicus made great strides in the field of astronomy. Copernicus realized that the earth was not the static center around which the rest of the universe revolved. Rather, the earth was a planet revolving around the sun. But Copernicus was reluctant to publish his findings. He knew the trouble he would have in convincing his contemporaries that people and the earth are not the center of all existence. He was right—the pride of the human race resisted clear evidence of this truth.

Man has always felt that he is the center and everything revolves around him. Our sinful nature doesn't want to accept the fact that the core of all truth is in God and not in man.

We hear people say, "I don't believe the Bible." Okay, but what do you base that conviction upon? "Well, nothing. I just feel that way." Then what *do* you believe? "I don't really know. I just don't think God would send people to hell."

People create an image of God based upon what they think is right, what they're comfortable with, or how they feel about it. What's amazing is that they don't see how foolish this is. *We* don't determine what God does—He is God! He's the center of the universe and the Creator and sustainer of all life. Who are we to tell Him how He should run our lives?

CONSEQUENCES OF FREEDOM

God has revealed Himself to the world—and now each of us must choose what we'll do about it. If that choice is to reject God in your life, He simply gives you over to what you've chosen above Him.

In our passage from Romans 1, Paul said three times, "God gave them up." What a tragic statement! He let them be enslaved to what they chose over Him: "God also gave them up to uncleanness, in the lusts of their hearts" (verse 24), "God gave them up to vile passions" (verse 26), and "God gave them over to a debased mind, to do those things which are not fitting" (verse 28). Can you think of a more dreadful state than for God to give us over to that which will utterly destroy us in time and for eternity? God gives us up…and steps back.

People are enamored with being free from any restraint; we steadfastly resist God telling us what to do. But when anyone chooses to exercise freedom to break God's laws, he's like a person who climbs to the top of a tall building and jumps off. On the way down, he feels great for the first several stories. There are no restraints, no restrictions, no hang-ups. But about ten stories before he hits the ground, he realizes that his choice of freedom is leading to some dire consequences he doesn't want to encounter. Can he reverse the falling process? Can he stop the fall? No. And for the final ten stories of his fall, he'll reexamine his prior definition of freedom—and realize it was wrong!

Once God steps back and leaves you to choose something other than Himself, a downward progression begins. There are many who put their hope in the mercy of God, the loving-kindness of God, the patience of God, or the grace of God—but fail to recognize that God shows His mercy, loving-kindness, patience, and grace to those who repent and turn from their sin. Those who refuse to turn to the truth of God remain under His wrath. He leaves them to suffer the consequence of their choice. "Do not be deceived, God is not mocked; for whatever a man sows, that he will also reap" (Galatians 6:7).

A SIMPLE CHOICE

But here's the good news: God has revealed Himself in much more than nature and in much more than our conscience in our inner being. He revealed Himself in Jesus Christ—to make clear once and for all how to have a relationship with God. For all who recognize their need for God and turn to Him, God will forgive their sin and cause their spiritual nature to be healed. They can start to relate to God as He intended from the very beginning.

How does this happen? Through experiencing the cross, the resurrection, and Pentecost.

Sin had to be removed before we could move toward our holy God. Sinful humanity cannot come into the presence of a holy God, so the holy God sent His Son, Jesus, to die on the cross to pay the penalty for your sin. He took your sin and died on your behalf.

Whereas the cross put to death your old life, the resurrection brings new life. The old life of sin cannot enter a holy place called heaven; new life in Christ is required. And this new

The cross put to death your old life, while the resurrection brings new life.

life of resurrection power is made a reality for us through the Holy Spirit.

And here's the most amazing thing about the gospel: the power of the cross and resurrection is just a prayer away. It's that simple. To be simple is not to be shallow or insignificant. To choose Christ is the most profound and substantial decision of your life.

You were created by God to know Him. Do you know Him? Are you seeking to know Him? If you choose to seek Him, you *will* find Him. You'll experience abundant life on earth…and for eternity, life everlasting.

CHAPTER 2

THE FATHER'S
ETERNAL PURPOSE

God was in Christ reconciling the world to Himself.
—2 CORINTHIANS 5:19

The gospel is a story about God's love. Many times we focus on the love of Christ and His sacrifice for our sins, but have you considered the love of *the Father* and *His* sacrifice for our sins?

The pain and suffering of Jesus are indeed beyond description...but the anguish in the heart of the Father was just as real.

Redemption of humanity was the *Father's* plan; it did not originate in the heart of Jesus. Jesus is portrayed in Scripture as the Suffering Servant who was obedient unto death. Who did He obey? *The Father.*

This is seen most clearly in the Garden of Gethsemane as Jesus looked toward the coming crucifixion and cried out, "O My

Father, if it is possible, let this cup pass from Me; nevertheless, not as I will, but as You will" (Matthew 26:39).

What Jesus faced on the eve of Calvary was not the carrying out of His own plan; it was the Father's plan, the Father's answer to man's problem of sin.

THE GOSPEL DISPLAYED

This eternal plan of the heavenly Father is what we call the gospel, the good news of Jesus. It is the central theme of Christianity. It defines who we are, and it describes the God we serve.

Its message is displayed in most traditional evangelical churches every time we gather for worship. Often there's an empty *cross* raised high and central in the sanctuary, symbolizing the completed work of the Atonement. There's often a *baptistery* right underneath the cross, symbolizing our identification with Christ as our Savior. There may be a *communion table* that's long and rectangular and decorated with flowers, leaving an image similar to that of a coffin or a grave and symbolizing the sacrifice of Christ's death. And there's a *pulpit,* where we proclaim the power of the gospel and the supremacy of God's Word.

Those visible symbols remind us of the Father's great plan of salvation. And although the proclamation of it is contemptible to the world, it's compelling for us. As Paul said, "The message of the cross is foolishness to those who are perishing, but to us who are being saved it is the power of God" (1 Corinthians 1:18).

The gospel story defines us as believers. If you don't understand the cross and resurrection, you don't understand the nature of God or what our faith is all about. We'll look later at the resurrec-

The gospel story defines us.

tion in the life of Jesus as well as its power in our lives, but first let's understand the resurrection in the heart of the Father.

A VIEW FROM ETERNITY

When we talk of the cross, we're looking at something much larger than the wooden timber that Jesus was nailed to on that fateful day. It's more than the nails, more than the crown of thorns, and more than the tomb.

Likewise, when we talk of the resurrection, we're looking at something more than a stone rolled away, empty burial wraps, and an angel's proclamation.

The cross and resurrection are the heavenly Father's plan to provide salvation for every person who ever walked this earth. It was in His heart from eternity. The Bible proclaims Jesus as the "Lamb slain *from the foundation of the world*" (Revelation 13:8). It talks of the "hope of eternal life which God, who cannot lie, promised *before time began*" (Titus 1:2).

We look back at the cross and resurrection with grateful hearts for what Jesus did on our behalf. But have you stopped to consider the cross from the Father's eternal perspective? What did the Father see from eternity that we're unable to comprehend?

Think again about this familiar verse: "For God so loved the world that He gave His only begotten Son, that whoever believes in Him should not perish but have everlasting life" (John 3:16).

What's the key word here? *Loved? Gave? Everlasting life?* We think it's the word *perish.* It's an awful word!

Think of it: God did not want us to perish. But from eternity's perspective, that's the destiny of all who are in sin: "At that time you were without Christ, being aliens from the commonwealth of Israel and strangers from the covenants of promise, having no hope and without God in the world" (Ephesians 2:12). Humanly speaking, all we could look forward to in eternity was our doom—and we could do nothing about it. We were all without hope, without God…and destined to perish. "But now in Christ Jesus you who once were far off have been brought near by the blood of Christ" (verse 13).

THAT DREADFUL WORD

There's something about that word *perish* that made the cross necessary, requiring God the Father to give His Son.

How serious is our sin?

From our perspective: "I'm a good person. I do my best. Sure I make mistakes, but I'm not that bad."

From God's perspective: "I gave My only begotten Son so that you would not *perish.*"

So we ask again: how serious is our sin? Serious enough for the Father to ordain His own Son to die a cruel death in our place.

In His life on this earth, Jesus was "holy, harmless, undefiled, separate from sinners" (Hebrews 7:26) and "without blemish and without spot" (1 Peter 1:19). "In Him was life, and the life was the light of men" (John 1:4). And yet, our sin necessitated His death. Our sin destined Christ to go to the cross. More than all the atrocities of man, the cruel death of Jesus on the cross tells best how serious sin is from God's perspective.

But still we argue: "I wasn't going against God. I just wasn't going with Him."

All sin has always been against God.

From God's perspective: "He who is not with Me is against Me, and he who does not gather with Me scatters abroad" (Matthew 12:30).

Before salvation, Paul described us as "enemies" of God (Colossians 1:21). All sin has always been *against* God, and He will not dismiss it lightly.

Throughout the Bible, the heavenly Father desires to cleanse His people of their sin that they may be an accurate reflection of

Him. If they're called by His name, they must reflect His nature—which is holy. He has been working to purify His people from the day Adam sinned in the Garden of Eden. His ultimate answer to the question of sin is found in the cross and resurrection, but He'd been working long before then to make us holy.

A HOLY STANDARD

If you want to know the heart of God to purify His people, consider this passage from the prophet Ezekiel. You'll see how much the Lord detests sin and is passionate about redemption.

> Therefore say to the house of Israel, "Thus says the Lord GOD: 'I do not do this for your sake, O house of Israel, but for My holy name's sake, which you have profaned among the nations wherever you went. And I will sanctify My great name, which has been profaned among the nations, which you have profaned in their midst; and the nations shall know that I am the LORD,' says the Lord GOD, 'when I am hallowed in you before their eyes. For I will take you from among the nations, gather you out of all countries, and bring you into your own land. Then I will sprinkle clean water on you, and you shall be clean; I will cleanse you from all your filthiness and from all your idols. I will give you a new heart and put a new spirit

within you; I will take the heart of stone out of your flesh and give you a heart of flesh. I will put My Spirit within you and cause you to walk in My statutes, and you will keep My judgments and do them. Then you shall dwell in the land that I gave to your fathers; you shall be My people, and I will be your God. I will deliver you from all your uncleannesses.'" (Ezekiel 36:22–29)

So how did God do it? How did He restore His name as holy among the nations? He sent His people into captivity in Babylon and destroyed Jerusalem and the temple. Because the people had profaned His name among the nations, He disciplined them before the nations so that all would see that sin is serious in God's eyes.

He is holy!

How should we look upon our sin today? How does God look upon our sin today? Our sin profanes His name—and the world is watching.

> *Our sin profanes God's name—and the world is watching.*

One of the great deterrents for people coming to God is sin among the people of God. "I don't want to go to church," people say. "It's full of hypocrites." Well, the church is not *full* of hypocrites, but there are *some* hypocrites, and Satan loves to showcase them to the world. These are people who profess to be Christians but act un-Christlike. They show a lack of mercy, of grace, of love, and of forgiveness. Some have taken the name of God yet live like the devil.

When the world sees no difference between one who claims to follow Christ and one who doesn't know Christ, His name is emptied of meaning.

CHOOSING HOLINESS

What should we expect God to do? Does the world need to know that He is holy?

Ask Him this: "Lord, is there anything in my life that misrepresents You to people who are watching? Has my life become a stumbling block to those who want to know You? Lord, cleanse my life and make me holy before a watching world."

If you ask the heavenly Father to make you holy before a watching world, He'll turn you to the cross and say, "Take a good look. This is My provision for your sin." The Father's plan to remove our sin was the death of Christ; His plan to free us from sin was the resurrection of Christ.

This was His plan from eternity. When Jesus was delivered into the hands of those who would kill Him, it was all "by the determined purpose and foreknowledge of God"; and the One whom they "crucified, and put to death" was also the One "whom *God raised up,* having loosed the pains of death, because it was not possible that He should be held by it" (Acts 2:23–24).

In the heart of God, the cross and resurrection were planned before all time, and it was out of His heart that the cross and resurrection came into this world's history: "*God* was in Christ reconciling the world to Himself" (2 Corinthians 5:19). "For *God* so loved the world that *He gave* His only begotten Son" (John 3:16).

And while this plan was being conceived in God's heart, He thought of you. Do you ever feel unloved? Don't! God expressed His love to you in the cross and resurrection. Love is not just words; it is action. Love *will be* expressed; it *must be* expressed. The cross and resurrection are God's expression of love to you. Christ Jesus gave His life to set you free from sin.

SACRIFICIAL LOVE

There's a story of a little boy whose sister needed a blood transfusion. The doctor explained that she had the same disease the boy had recovered from two years earlier. Her only chance for recovery was a transfusion from someone who'd previously conquered the disease. Since the two children had the same rare blood type, the boy was the ideal donor.

"Would you give your blood to Mary?" the doctor asked.

Johnny hesitated. His lower lip started to tremble. After a moment of serious contemplation, he smiled and said, "Sure, for my sister."

Soon the two children were wheeled into the hospital room. Mary was pale and thin; Johnny was robust and healthy. Neither spoke, but when their eyes met, Johnny grinned. As the nurse inserted the needle into his arm, Johnny's smile began to fade. He watched the blood flow through the tube.

When the ordeal was almost over, his voice, slightly shaky, broke the silence. "Doctor, when do I die?"

Only then did the doctor realize why Johnny had hesitated, why his lip had trembled when he agreed to donate his blood. The boy thought that giving his blood to his sister meant giving up his life. In that brief moment, he made his great decision.

Johnny, fortunately, didn't have to die to save his sister. Each of us, however, has a condition far more serious than Mary's, and it required Jesus to give not just His blood, but His life.

Hear again this truth: "God so loved the world that He gave His only begotten Son, that whoever believes in Him should not perish but have everlasting life" (John 3:16).

Trusting in Christ's death will bring the power of the resurrection to bear upon our lives and keep us from falling into sin.

Could you do what the heavenly Father did? Could you give your son for those who were your enemies? That's exactly what the Father did. The Father's suffering was real. His sacrifice was great. And if there had been any other way to cleanse your life and keep you from perishing, He would have done it.

How serious is your sin? Do you still think it isn't that bad? Are you still living in sin? Each one of us must put our trust in Jesus, who died on the cross to take away our sin. That decision will bring the power of the resurrection to bear upon our lives and keep us from falling into sin.

A FATHER'S LOVE

Do you still think of God only as a harsh judge who condemns? Or have you considered the Father's love for you, that He sent His Son to pay the price for your sin? "What then shall we say to these things? If God is for us, who can be against us? He who did not spare His own Son, but delivered Him up for us all, how shall He not with Him also freely give us all things?" (Romans 8:31–32). This is the God we serve. He sent His Son to die on the cross for our sin. He raised His Son to new life in the resurrection to give us new life—abundant life in Christ.

Remember, the resurrection is something the Father did, not the Son. The Son chose to be obedient unto death, but He couldn't choose to resurrect Himself from the grave. He left Himself in the hands of the Father with absolute confidence; the promise of the Father would be fulfilled in the resurrection.

Have you ever noticed the focus in Peter's sermon on the Day of Pentecost, as recorded in Acts 2? Peter's primary emphasis is on the work of God, not on Jesus.

This is not what you would expect. Peter was a disciple of Jesus. He had walked with his Lord for more than three years. Jesus was not only his Lord; He was Peter's best friend. And Peter had seen the gospel story unfold before his very eyes. He watched the miracles, he was instructed by His inspired teaching, he witnessed the crucifixion, and he was transformed by the resurrection. You would therefore think that Peter's sermon would be on the work of Christ to set people free. But it was not. Peter talked about God's work *through* the life of Christ. Of course, Jesus is prominent in the sermon, but listen to how Peter talks of the relationship between the Father and Son:

> Men of Israel, hear these words: Jesus of Nazareth, a Man *attested by God* to you by miracles, wonders, and signs which *God did through Him* in your midst, as you yourselves also know—Him, being delivered by the *determined purpose and foreknowledge of God,* you have taken by lawless hands, have crucified, and put to death; whom *God raised up,* having loosed the pains of death, because it was not possible that He should be held by it.… This Jesus *God has raised up,* of which we are all witnesses. (Acts 2:22–24, 32)

Can you see the eternal purpose of the Father in the death and resurrection of the Son? Make no mistake: Jesus fulfilled the will of His Father. And it was the Father's eternal purpose that we be saved from eternally perishing by the death and resurrection of the Lamb of God, Jesus Christ.

The Son *had* to die; the Father *had* to raise Him from the dead.

PART TWO

The Resurrection in the Life of the Lord Jesus

CHAPTER 3

THE REALITY OF SIN: HE DIED

He made Him who knew no sin to be sin for us, that
we might become the righteousness of God in Him.
—2 CORINTHIANS 5:21

The resurrection of Jesus was necessary because of the simple fact that He died. So to fully understand the meaning of the resurrection, we must first seek to better understand what it means that Jesus died.

Let's consider two simple but important questions: *Why did Christ die?* and *What does this have to do with me?* We'll never understand resurrection power until we first deal with these questions. Resurrection power follows death; it's built upon the sacrifice Jesus made on the cross. And though it happened two thousand years ago, it has everything to do with our lives today.

GOD IS TRUSTWORTHY

Before we answer these two questions, let's establish some basic assumptions. First, let's agree that God knows more than we do. Second, whatever He does, it's always right. And third, God knows something about our lives that we desperately need to know.

These assumptions are the basis upon which we'll approach the two questions above. We could look for answers in many different places, but what's at stake is too important to get it wrong. The questions we're considering will impact our lives for eternity. So we'll seek to fully answer the questions from God's Word, trusting that He's the only One who knows the truth about the death and resurrection of Christ.

Only God knows the truth about the death and resurrection of Christ.

Back to the question, *Why did Christ die?* Was it because He was trapped, arrested, and crucified? No, the Bible testifies that Jesus willingly laid down His life; He affirmed that nobody could take His life from Him (John 10:15–18).

Did He die so that we can have eternal life? While it's true that Christ's death and resurrection provide salvation, that speaks to the result of His death, not the reason for it.

So why did He choose to die? Why couldn't He just forgive our sin and be done with it? If it's true that God loves us equally, regardless of our condition, and our salvation does not depend upon our being worthy but is available to all who accept it, why the cross? Why all the words like *sacrifice, redemption, propitiation, reconciliation,* and *atonement*?

The reason Christ had to die was that *sin is real and present in this world,* and *the wages of sin is death.*

The angel told Joseph as much before Jesus was even born: "She [Mary] will bring forth a Son, and you shall call His name JESUS, for *He will save His people from their sins*" (Matthew 1:21). The wages of sin is death, and someone had to pay the price.

What does that have to do with you? Everything! It was for *your* sin He died. He was born that He might die for your sin and clothe you with His righteousness, giving you access to a relationship with a holy God. "For when we were still without strength, in due time Christ died for the ungodly" (Romans 5:6).

It isn't hard to convince people they're sinners, for we all know that we've sinned. We all know our mistakes, our poor choices, our ungodly thoughts, and our selfish desires. What we don't grasp is how truly offensive that sin is to God or how to be free from that sin in order to live lives pleasing to God.

OVERCOMING OUR SIN

The reality of sin in this world is why Jesus came here. His death and resurrection are for the purpose of resolving the problem of sin and providing people the opportunity to enter into a relationship with God. "Christ died for the *ungodly*" (Romans 5:6)—that statement is at the heart of the gospel and applies to every human being. And we can't grow in appreciating the resurrection without a deeper grasp of what it means that Christ died for the ungodly.

Although the death and resurrection of Christ represent the turning point of all human history—the epicenter from which the power of God is released to mankind—Satan is good at keeping us from understanding these things. He misdirects us with partial truths that keep us from experiencing the gospel's full impact here and now.

Our own hope of resurrection is not just a future event that occurs when we physically die and are transported into heaven; its impact is meant for today. When the Bible speaks of resurrection, especially as it applies to our own lives, it's almost always in reference to the power to overcome the sin that's within us. But in heaven there is no sin. So our foremost benefit of resurrection power is not for when we get to heaven, but to help us here on earth.

> *Our foremost benefit of resurrection power is not for when we get to heaven, but to help us here on earth.*

Scripture makes this clear. Consider these statements from the apostle Paul:

How shall we who died to sin live any longer in it? Or
do you not know that as many of us as were baptized
into Christ Jesus were baptized into His death? Therefore we were buried with Him through baptism into
death, that *just as Christ was raised from the dead* by the
glory of the Father, even *so we also should walk in newness of life.* For if we have been united together in the
likeness of His death, certainly we also shall be in the
likeness of His resurrection, knowing this, that our old
man was crucified with Him, that the body of sin might
be done away with, that we should no longer be slaves
of sin. For he who has died has been freed from sin.
Now if we died with Christ, we believe that we shall
also live with Him, knowing that Christ, having been
raised from the dead, dies no more. Death no longer
has dominion over Him. For the death that He died,
He died to sin once for all; but the life that He lives,
He lives to God. Likewise you also, reckon yourselves to
be dead indeed to sin, but alive to God in Christ Jesus
our Lord. (Romans 6:2–11)

Can you see the connection? Jesus died for the sin of the
world and was raised to conquer sin's destructive power. And all
who have been resurrected with Him are no longer under the

dominion of sin and death. They are now alive to God and are no longer slaves to sin, but walk in newness of life.

Resurrection power is to free us from sin today and forevermore!

This is why we cannot fully realize the power of the resurrection until we've understood what Christ was resurrected *from*—the death grip of sin. Christ's cruel murder at the hands of sinners was not the primary action of what happened on the cross. The darkest part of the crucifixion was what happened in His soul as the sin of the world was laid upon Him. And when we think of Jesus crucified and buried, Satan wants us to misunderstand what really happened on the cross, as well as the power of the resurrection that followed. For on that cross, sin was dealt with once and for all, while the resurrection was the final stripping of sin's death grip, a blow that echoed throughout eternity.

POWER OF DECEPTION

If you're a Christian, Satan has absolutely no power over you. But he's a liar. He holds the lethal weapon of deception. And he has lots of bells and whistles to distract you from seeing what will damn you and what will set you free.

When it comes to the cross and the resurrection of Christ, Satan will try to keep your focus on a body that was beaten, whipped, pierced, and crucified. He doesn't mind you thinking about the agony of intense pain, the public humiliation, and the innocent blood that Christ shed. He isn't bothered if you see the truth of the crucifixion—as long as you don't notice *the truth of His death.*

Satan isn't bothered if you see the truth of the crucifixion--as long as you don't notice the truth of Christ's death.

Paul warns us, "But I fear, lest somehow, as the serpent deceived Eve by his craftiness, so your minds may be corrupted from the simplicity that is in Christ" (2 Corinthians 11:3). Christ is the key to understanding how God saved us through the cross and resurrection.

Paul said, "God demonstrates His own love toward us, in that while we were still sinners, Christ died for us" (Romans 5:8). When Christ died for us, it wasn't because we were human, but because we were sinners. And Christ's death on our behalf was not primarily about our physical bodies, but about our souls that were already dead in sin. For our own "death" is not primarily a matter of the body; it's the plight of our souls.

LIFE AND DEATH

Every time the Lord talked about life and death, you sense that He's talking about something other than what we would ordinarily think. When bodily activity ceases, we call it "death"; but Jesus was always referring to that kind of death as "sleep."

Take for example the daughter of Jairus, a synagogue ruler. He came to Jesus saying, "My little daughter lies at the point of *death*. Come and lay Your hands on her, that she may be healed, and she will live" (Mark 5:23). Jesus went with Jairus to the man's house, but on their way they were met by a servant of Jairus who told him, "Your daughter is *dead*" (verse 35). At the house they "saw a tumult and those who wept and wailed loudly" (verse 38) because this girl had physically died. But Jesus made a startling statement: "The child is *not dead, but sleeping*" (verse 39). Then He walked inside and proceeded to give physical life back to the girl, and she arose.

Or consider Jesus' friend Lazarus of Bethany, whom Jesus raised to life after he'd been dead four days and sealed in a tomb. Before going to Bethany, Jesus said, "Our friend Lazarus sleeps, but I go that I may wake him up" (John 11:11). "Waking up" Lazarus meant bringing him back to physical life and restoring him to his family, just as Jesus had done with the daughter of Jairus.

To bring back to life those who were physically dead was no great challenge for Jesus. He would simply speak, and they would arise. He almost casually refers to their condition as "sleep" because He had the ability to awake them, giving life by the command of His voice.

Jesus reserved the word *death* to express an experience infinitely more significant. And to fully appreciate the *life* Christ has given us, we need to better understand the *death* from which He saved us. To better understand the magnitude of resurrection power, we must see more clearly what happened at the cross and the nature of Christ's death.

So before we look further at resurrection life, we must see that contrast.

BELIEVERS CANNOT DIE

Having come to this earth from eternity, Jesus had the correct "big picture" of life and death that none of us on earth ever naturally possess. He came to help us see *from His perspective* the reality of our life and the reality of our death—to see these in a way that the world cannot understand. When He speaks, He's speaking pure truth from an eternal perspective.

From this viewpoint, Jesus tells us, "Most assuredly, I say to you, if anyone keeps My word he shall *never see death*" (John 8:51). This startling statement goes against everything human existence has ever experienced. But we are to base truth not on our experience, but on the Word of God.

Consider another significant passage. In a lengthy discussion with a crowd in Galilee about "bread from heaven," Jesus boldly stated, "I am the bread of life.… This is the bread which comes down from heaven, that one may eat of it and *not die*" (John 6:32, 48, 50).

Or as He said earlier to a crowd in Jerusalem, "Most assuredly, I say to you, he who hears My word and believes in Him who sent Me *has everlasting life,* and shall not come into judgment, but *has passed from death into life*" (John 5:24).

Or as He told the sister of Lazarus before raising him from the dead, "Whoever lives and believes in Me *shall never die*" (John 11:26).

To believe in Jesus is to pass out of death and into life. To believe in Jesus is to possess everlasting life and to never die.

Jesus clearly uses the terms "life" and "death" differently than we use them.

According to Jesus, before anyone believes in Him, that person is *dead.* Then once he or she becomes a Christian, that person is alive forevermore.

Clearly, Jesus uses the terms *life* and *death* differently than we use them.

JESUS DID DIE

Although Jesus uses the word *sleep* for what we think of as physical death, take careful note: Jesus did not come to save us from sleep, but to deliver us from *death.* All human beings—saints and sinners alike—will "sleep" (physically die), but we will not all die.

And when Scripture says that "Christ *died*" (and it often does, as in Romans 5:6–8; 1 Corinthians 15:3; and Galatians 2:21), it's referring to more than "sleep"—He actually died. On the cross,

He experienced more than just the cessation of physical life. He died in the eternal sense of the word. If He had experienced only the physical death of His body, He would have referred to that ordeal as "sleep." Perhaps we too ought to reserve the word *death* for something different than just the physical termination of life.

So what did Jesus experience when He "died"? What really happened on that awful hill called Mount Calvary? And what new "life" came from the resurrection?

We believe that the true death of Jesus began at Gethsemane, on the night when He was praying. We read how Jesus went there and "began to be sorrowful and deeply distressed"; He turned to His disciples and told them, "My soul is exceedingly sorrowful, *even to death.* Stay here and watch with Me" (Matthew 26:37–38). He had not yet begun to "sleep"—to physically die—but He'd begun the process of dying.

Was Jesus afraid of the cross? Not at all; He doesn't fear "sleep." But true death was soon approaching. The sin of the world was about to be placed on His shoulders, and He was headed to the cross to die for your sin and my sin. Why? Because the wages of sin is "death."

At Calvary, as Jesus hung on the cross, He made this statement: "My God, My God, why have You forsaken Me?" (Matthew 27:46). That was true *death*—even before the termination of His physical life. "Sleep" would soon follow, but He'd already entered a place He'd never entered before.

Jesus had never sinned; He was the perfect Son of God. But because the sin of the world was placed upon Him, and the wages of sin is death, the Son's relationship with the Father was struck a deathblow. For the first time in His eternal existence, He was in spiritual darkness. The sight of the Father's house was now obscured. The Father's hand was withdrawn.

Jesus was in utter darkness. He was suffering the agonizing loneliness of sin that separates humans from a holy God. For that homelessness of the soul—that separation from the heavenlies into outer darkness—is the wages of sin.

Sin Is Death

Though Christ had known no sin, He died for the ungodly. He died for you and me. He tasted death for every person. And the Bible states that we, apart from Christ, are still under the dominion of that law of sin and death (Romans 7:23–24).

Sin brings death, abandonment, homelessness of the soul, and utter darkness (Matthew 8:12). That's the state of every soul apart from Christ: "For all have sinned and fall short of the glory of God" (Romans 3:23). And if we choose to neglect Christ and His death for our sin, turn our backs on His grace, and live without Christ in our lives, we will surely die—no, we're already dead. We're already separated from the Father. Our souls are dead, and the great Day of Judgment will only reveal the fact that our souls are homeless, desolate, and separated by a great chasm from the presence of God. Everyone like this shall go out into great darkness, into a night of loneliness, and into eternal death.

Yes, we use these terms *life* and *death* much differently from the way Jesus uses them. But let us say this again: Jesus came down to earth out of eternity and ascended back to the Father—He knows what He's talking about! So when we explore resurrection life and its power to transform, we need to rearrange our thinking into a whole new dimension

> *To explore resurrection power, we need to rearrange our thinking into a whole new dimension.*

that goes beyond the physical into the realm of the spiritual, where our souls dwell.

RESURRECTION IS LIFE

As we noted earlier, resurrection power doesn't start when we physically die and are transported into a new home in heaven. There's a dimension to the resurrection that we experience the moment we believe in Jesus. This is sometimes referred to with the phrase "already, but not yet." Believers already experience the power of the resurrection, though they'll experience it in a fuller way when Christ returns.

We've already talked about that word *perish* in John 3:16. Not only did the Father know what it means for us to eternally perish; Jesus also knew what that word means. And because He understood what *perish* really involves, it thrust Him forward to the cross.

That's why we read, "From that time Jesus began to show to His disciples that He *must* go to Jerusalem, and suffer many things from the elders and chief priests and scribes, and be killed, and be raised the third day" (Matthew 16:21).

He *must* go to Jerusalem and die on our behalf—so that those who believe in Him would never die, never taste eternal death, and never experience what it means to perish, but instead have everlasting life. Jesus knew that *He* must go, for nobody else fulfilled the requirements of justification. The price for sin and eternal punishment could not be paid with material possessions, for they too will all pass away. It could not be paid with the blood of bulls and goats or any other temporary, soulless creature (Hebrews 10:4). And it could not be paid by any other human being, for all of us have sinned and fall short.

No, the price had to be paid by the "precious blood of Christ, as of a lamb without blemish and without spot" (1 Peter 1:19).

According to Scripture, before we knew God, we were dead. Once we put our faith in Christ, we came to life. And at the cross we leave our sin that caused the separation. For our sin *is* death. It is that which keeps us from life, a wall that cannot be overcome.

We hear Paul crying out, "O wretched man that I am! Who

will deliver me from this...*death*?" (Romans 7:24). Then comes the answer: "There is therefore now no condemnation to those who are in Christ Jesus, who do not walk according to the flesh, but according to the Spirit. For the law of the Spirit of *life* in Christ Jesus has made me free from the law of *sin and death*" (8:1–2).

Unless we go to the cross with the Lord and are saved from our sins, we cannot live. Death is still hovering over our soul, for sin remains.

THE BARRIER OF SIN REMOVED

Because of what Christ has done for us, the barrier between us and God is no longer sin.

The good news is almost unbelievable: no matter how deep and ugly our sin, Christ's sacrifice is much greater. God's provision for sin far exceeds our worst rebellion. The only thing to keep you from a relationship with God is no longer sin but your refusal to come to Him in repentance. He has forever taken care of your sin; Christ has already paid the price for sin; He died for all that we might live.

> *The good news is almost unbelievable: no matter how deep and ugly our sin, Christ's sacrifice is much greater.*

The only thing now keeping us from a relationship with God

is our will, refusing to believe and accept God's provision for us in Christ. That barrier is overcome when we choose to step out in faith and receive Him.

This is not an elusive doctrine; it's a reality to live out in daily life. Your life today is the sum total of the choices you've made. And when it comes to salvation, Jesus is the only choice, the only answer.

Some people have the idea that physical realities are the real world while the spiritual realm is some kind of effervescent concept that remains elusive in day-to-day living. But from Jesus' perspective, spiritual life is reality and physical life can distract us, pull us away, and keep us from seeing what will last for eternity.

So we must take His words by faith and move beyond those physical distractions. We must make the choice to believe what Christ has said and to live in the reality of the risen Lord. And then we come to experience how the resurrection in its essence is freedom from sin.

THE GIFT OF LIFE RECEIVED

In 1829, a Pennsylvania man named George Wilson, together with an accomplice, robbed a U.S. mail carrier, endangering the mail carrier's life in the process. Both men soon were captured, brought to trial, and found guilty. In those days of stricter punishment, both were sentenced to be hanged.

The accomplice was hanged in 1830, but Wilson had influential friends who took action on his behalf. They got the attention of President Andrew Jackson, who granted Wilson a pardon less than a month before the scheduled execution.

Imagine how relieved you would feel if you were sentenced to be hanged, then received a presidential pardon. George Wilson, however, refused it—and the authorities didn't know what to do. How could they go through with hanging a man when his presidential pardon was sitting on their desk?

The matter eventually reached the Supreme Court. In the court's ruling, Chief Justice John Marshall stated, "A pardon is an act of grace"; and when such a pardon is delivered to someone, "delivery is not complete, without acceptance. It may then be rejected by the person to whom it is tendered"; and if it were rejected, then there was "no power in a court to force it on him."

So George Wilson was hanged—even though "an act of grace" on his behalf had pardoned him.

How will we respond to the act of grace that has pardoned us from eternal death?

We all have sinned, we all are condemned, we all are spiritually dead. But because of Christ's death and resurrection, we have a choice: either remain in sin and death or choose the power of God to set us free.

Christ died for the ungodly—and that word *ungodly* includes each one of us. We deserve death. But Christ has granted us the gift of salvation. The pardon from sin is on the desk. We must choose to receive this gift. And receiving it isn't just a one-time act, but a daily decision to walk in the power of the resurrection and experience new life in Christ.

CHAPTER 4

THE REALITY OF SALVATION: HE ROSE

The last enemy that will be destroyed is death.
—1 CORINTHIANS 15:26

People have always been haunted by the thought of death. But now that Christ has been resurrected, there's no need to fear death anymore. Death has lost its sting; we can escape everlasting punishment for sin and, with it, eternal separation from God.

Physical death is now but a transition into our new and glorious existence in God's presence; it's the shedding of our weak and frail bodies and the receiving of new resurrection bodies. That is, *if* we choose to accept the gift of salvation, to repent of our sin, and to make Christ the Lord of our lives.

HISTORICAL RESURRECTION

Our resurrection life hinges on the fact that Jesus really did rise from the dead to new life. And if that fact isn't established, our faith is in vain.

So *did* Jesus rise? Did He truly die and then come back to life? This is a valid question that must be addressed.

The fact that Jesus lived has been clearly established. He's not a figment of the imagination but a historical person. No educated person contests this fact; Jews, Muslims, and atheists all believe as a fact of history that Jesus lived. So there's no need to argue this point. But many deny that the historical Jesus was the divine Son of God, and they deny He rose from the dead.

There are many approaches to answering such objections. Before we consider a quite unique and rather unexpected approach to this which we find in Scripture, let's approach the issue from a purely historical examination.

JESUS DIED

Jesus died on the cross. This needs to be established because some argue that Jesus didn't actually experience physical death on the cross. They suggest that He passed out, then later woke up in the tomb and walked out. They suppose that after all the torture and physical suffering He went through, He awoke from His stupor, unwrapped Himself from the burial wrappings, rolled away the stone, and left.

Not likely! But for those looking for a rational explanation, they'll even hold on to the irrational rather than accept the miraculous.

Is it possible that Jesus didn't actually experience physical death on the cross?

The physical suffering Jesus endured left Him in a physical condition of injury and trauma that was inescapable. His suffering began in the Garden of Gethsemane, where His sweat became like drops of blood, a detail recorded by the physician Luke in Luke 22:44. Jesus endured a medical condition known as hematidrosis, in which tiny capillaries in the sweat glands rupture, causing the skin to be extremely fragile and sensitive to the touch. This condition is rare but has been known to occur when a person is suffering under extreme amounts of stress.

Shortly thereafter, Jesus was arrested, then questioned in a series of "trials" that lasted through the night. He was whipped with a cat-o'-nine-tails that would have torn open the skin of His back (John 19:1). Soldiers pressed down upon His head a crown of thorns that would have cut deeply into His scalp (verse 2). He was beaten at the hands of the Roman soldiers (verse 3). Then they placed a heavy cross upon His back as they led Him to Golgotha (verse 17). It was there that the soldiers nailed Him to that cross with thick iron spikes in His hands and feet (verse 18). And the world watched as His tortured body hung there for hours for all to see. The word *excruciating*—which literally means "out of the cross"—is a fitting description of the ordeal of crucifixion.

After such an ordeal, can you imagine Jesus having the strength to loosen Himself from under a hundred pounds of burial spices (verse 39), unwrap Himself from the linen strips that tightly bound Him (verse 40), and roll away the stone that sealed His tomb (20:1)? Neither can we.

Others say that Jesus never made it to the tomb, but orchestrated an elaborate plan to make it *appear* as though He died and rose again. Perhaps He had a twin; perhaps they substituted Judas; perhaps the sponge filled with sour wine given to Jesus on the cross was really a sedative that made Him sleep; perhaps the soldiers were paid off to lie about His death. Perhaps…

People who don't want to believe that Jesus is the Son of God will conjecture anything to try to disprove His death and resurrection.

The enemies of Jesus, however, proved that He really died. They verified His death. A crowd of people witnessed the entire ordeal (John 19:20). A Roman soldier pierced His side on the cross, causing water and blood to come out (verse 34). The blood had started to separate, signifying that physical death had already occurred. A centurion, a man well acquainted with the signs of death, verified that Jesus

The enemies of Jesus proved that He really died.

was dead (Luke 23:47). There was no doubt in the executioners' minds that Jesus was dead.

The friends of Jesus agreed. Joseph of Arimathea and Nicodemus took the body of Jesus and prepared it for burial; they knew He had died. Disciples who didn't want to believe He was gone were absolutely convinced He had died.

Jesus was crucified…and He *died* on the cross.

JESUS WAS BURIED

After Jesus died, He was quickly prepared for burial and then laid in the tomb that belonged to Joseph of Arimathea (Matthew 27:57–60).

Some concede this fact, but then argue that His disciples stole the body of Jesus and propagated the myth of resurrection.

But again, His enemies ensured that this couldn't happen. The body of Jesus was placed in a tomb that was then closed off with a huge rock and sealed by Roman soldiers. The seal was a cord placed across the tomb with wax over the cord. The Roman seal was imprinted in the wax, and Roman soldiers were placed by the tomb to guarantee that nobody stole the body. They knew it was predicted that Jesus would rise after three days, and they didn't want His disciples to steal the body and cause an uprising (Matthew 27:63–66). The enemies of Jesus ensured that Jesus would stay in the tomb and that nobody was going to take away the body.

They did a good job; *nobody* stole Jesus' body from the tomb.

THE EMPTY TOMB

Jesus died and was buried, yet three days later His tomb was empty. Not many argue this point. Everyone recognizes that *something* happened to the body. For on the Sunday after Passover, some women went to put spices in the tomb and found the stone rolled away and the tomb empty. Jesus wasn't there. But they didn't understand what had happened and surmised that somebody had taken the body (John 20:2).

These women were "Mary Magdalene, Joanna, Mary the mother of James, and the other women with them" (Luke 24:10). They went back and reported to the disciples what they had seen. The disciples were also startled and couldn't believe the body was gone. They had to see this for themselves.

Peter and John ran to the tomb. Inside they saw the linen burial clothes—not ripped open or stolen away with the body, but lying there in an orderly manner (John 20:6–7). The body had not been stolen but had passed through the clothes...and was alive.

If the physical evidence wasn't enough, God sent angels to explain it (Matthew 28:5–7; Mark 16:5–7; Luke 24:4–7; John

20:12). So the resurrection was confirmed not only by physical evidence but also by divine messengers.

JESUS APPEARED

It was also confirmed by many personal appearances of the risen Lord—the most convincing evidence of all. The disciples saw Jesus alive for themselves.

Still, some argue that the disciples only *thought* they saw Jesus; it was actually an illusion or a daydream. But this so-called illusion was far too widespread to be an imaginary vision.

Jesus was seen on the day of resurrection by Mary Magdalene (John 20:14–17), ten disciples in the upper room (verses 19–23), and two disciples on the road to Emmaus (Luke 24:13–31). Eight days later, Jesus was seen by Thomas and the other ten disciples, again in the upper room (John 20:24–29). A short while later, Jesus was seen by the disciples on the shore of the Sea of Galilee (21:1–14). He was also seen by a crowd of disciples as He ascended into heaven, forty days after Passover (Acts 1:3–11).

The resurrected Jesus was seen by many people on many different occasions. This had to be real.

Paul later records that the resurrected Jesus was seen by Peter and the disciples, by His brother James, and by more than five hundred people at one time (1 Corinthians 15:5–7).

Jesus was seen in many places, by many people, on many different occasions. This had to be real and no illusion; the same daydream doesn't happen to hundreds of people at the same time!

DRAMATIC CHANGE

No one will argue that the resurrection didn't cause some dramatic changes in the lives of Jesus' followers. It's undeniable.

One of those changes, which might not appear significant to many, is how the disciples changed the day of worship from Saturday to Sunday. The Sabbath day was Saturday, the day God rested after six days of creation. Honoring the Sabbath was a part of Mosaic law, the fourth of the Ten Commandments: "Remember the Sabbath day, to keep it holy. Six days you shall labor and do all your work, but the seventh day is the Sabbath of the LORD your God" (Exodus 20:8–10). And yet Sunday, rather than Saturday, became the Sabbath for the early church.

Jesus had already indicated His own authority over the Sabbath: "The Sabbath was made for man, and not man for the Sabbath. Therefore the Son of Man is also Lord of the Sabbath" (Mark 2:27–28). He centered the Sabbath on Himself, and by so doing He extended the Sabbath from just a Jewish practice to something experienced by the entire world—Gentiles included.

So when the Christians of the early church chose Sunday as

their day for gathering to worship, the choice was centered on Christ's resurrection and its universal message.

The biblical record for this change for the Sabbath is found in 1 Corinthians 16:2, where Paul gave instructions on gathering "on the first day of the week" in order to collect an offering, and in Acts 20:7, which mentions "the first day of the week, when the disciples came together to break bread."

Whereas the Jews functioned under the Law, believers in Jesus now live in grace. Grace and truth came in the person of Jesus, and through His resurrection we now live this new life. Resurrection day, Sunday, is now the day of worship for those who have put their faith in Christ.

THE DISCIPLES' ULTIMATE SACRIFICE

Perhaps the greatest change caused by the resurrection was in the character of the disciples. They had previously been timid, afraid, and depressed after witnessing the arrest and suffering of Jesus. But after His resurrection they became aggressive, bold, and full of joy.

Peter is a prime example. He was the one who had earlier denied the Lord to a lowly servant girl. But after the resurrection, he stood in the temple courts defying the very men who put Jesus on the cross (Acts 4:20).

When you observe the post-resurrection disciples, you see that they had *life*! Their circumstances didn't matter. They had joy in the midst of suffering and peace in the midst of turmoil. Nothing could take away their passion arising from the everlasting life they'd received from Christ.

For the post-resurrection disciples, nothing could take away their passion.

The disciples believed so much in the resurrection that they gave their lives to sharing the news. The first to die was James the brother of John, who was killed by the sword upon the order of King Herod (Acts 12:1–2). Church tradition holds that John miraculously survived being put into a cauldron of boiling water, then later was exiled to the island of Patmos; Peter was crucified in Rome upside down; Matthew was slain by a sword in a distant city in Ethiopia; James the son of Alphaeus was thrown from a pinnacle of the temple, then beaten to death with a blacksmith's tool; Philip was hanged against a pillar at Hierapolis in Phrygia; Bartholomew was skinned alive; Andrew was bound to a cross—and preached to his persecutors until he died; Thomas was run through with a lance in the East Indies; Jude was shot to death with arrows; Matthias was first stoned and then beheaded; Mark died in Alexandria in Egypt after being cruelly dragged through the city.

Let me ask you: Would you have died for a lie? Would these disciples have endured such persecution for a dead man?

No. They saw the risen Lord—then gave their very lives in

service to Him. They were no longer afraid of death because they'd found the true meaning of life. They were transformed, for they were living in resurrection life.

PETER'S EVIDENCE

So we see ample historical evidence for the resurrection.[3]

Earlier we mentioned a unique and rather unexpected approach to the resurrection that we find in Scripture. Let's go back and explore it.

How did Peter explain the resurrection on the Day of Pentecost? He was a close disciple of Jesus, he had been there to witness the crucifixion, and he'd talked with Jesus after He rose from the dead.

But in his Pentecost sermon, Peter didn't give such factual evidence. He didn't say, "I know God raised Him up again because I saw Him." Instead he declared, "I know God raised Him up because *it was impossible for Him to be held in death's grip.*" This is recorded in Peter's words in Acts 2:24, where Jesus is referred to as the One "whom God raised up, having loosed the pains of death, because it was not possible that He should be held by it."

Peter's words present the first apostolic statement on the resurrection. Peter was declaring with absolute certainty, "God raised up Jesus—the man you nailed to a cross."

Remember that Peter was speaking to a crowd in Jerusalem,

the city where Jesus died. Many in that crowd had probably been eyewitnesses to Jesus' crucifixion, which had happened there less than two months earlier. His execution had been a prominent event in the city, one that no doubt was a topic of discussion for a long time. Peter was addressing people keenly interested in what he was talking about.

In Peter's words to them, the resurrection was just as much a fact of history as the crucifixion—a fact with immediate and powerful results. And the reason Peter gave for the resurrection is simply this: it wasn't possible that Jesus could be held by death.

Peter declared the impossibility of Jesus' being held by death.

The world today says, "It's impossible for Jesus to rise from the dead." But Peter said, "It's impossible for Jesus *not* to rise from the dead."

How could Peter make such a statement? His argument is based not upon the kind of factual evidence we would think of, but upon two other points.

First, Peter bases it on the nature of biblical prophecy. In stating that it was impossible for death to hold Jesus, Peter noted that David spoke "concerning Him" (Acts 2:25). Christ's resurrection had already been prophesied. And once God speaks, it is done. Jesus *must* rise again because God's Word is always true; He cannot be wrong. Once the prophetic word is given, God's nature is such that He cannot fail to fulfill it.

Peter quotes Psalm 16 and says that David was speaking of Christ when he said, "You will not leave my soul in Hades, nor will You allow Your Holy One to see corruption" (Acts 2:27).

Peter was whispering into the souls of the Jews standing before him, for Jews knew that once God spoke through a prophet, it was as good as done.

Of course, Christ's resurrection was foretold not only by Old Testament prophets, but by the Lord Himself, as we've already seen: "Jesus began to show to His disciples that He must go to Jerusalem, and suffer many things from the elders and chief priests and scribes, and be killed, and be raised the third day" (Matthew 16:21). Divine prophecy is a guarantee that death couldn't hold Jesus in the grave.

There's also another reason Peter could present the resurrection as fact. Peter was referring to the very meaning of life itself. He bases this argument on the nature of Christ. Because of who Christ is, it's impossible that death could hold Him in the grave. Peter was convinced that *life* was the nature of Jesus. Peter would later speak of Jesus as "the Holy One and the Just" and "*the Prince of life,* whom God raised from the dead, of which we are witnesses" (Acts 3:14–15). Jesus is that Prince of life, and without Him, there is no life—not for anyone. It was impossible for Jesus to remain in death because He is life itself. He *must* burst forth from the grave or deny His very nature as the Prince of life.

Peter's understanding of Christ's nature is in keeping with

what the other disciples had come to know. The apostle John, for example, opened his gospel by stating, "In Him was *life,* and the life was the light of men" (John 1:4).

Jesus Himself made this teaching very clear. He said to Mary and Martha, "*I am the resurrection and the life.* He who believes in Me, though he may die, he shall live" (11:25). And He said to His disciples, "*I am* the way, the truth, and *the life.* No one comes to the Father except through Me" (14:6).

Jesus said more about His "life" nature in these words:

> For as the Father has life in Himself, so He has granted
> the Son to have life in Himself, and has given Him
> authority to execute judgment also, because He is
> the Son of Man. Do not marvel at this; for the hour is
> coming in which all who are in the graves will hear His
> voice and come forth." (5:26–29)

Jesus says that the Father—who "has *life in Himself* "—has also given to Jesus "*life in Himself.*" And this life isn't something that anyone could ever take away from Him, for Jesus *is* life; He is self-existent over and above that which we call death. He lives forever because He *is* life and has become the source of life for all who believe in Him.

Earlier we warned of how Satan tries to keep us from seeing the truth. And God's truth includes this: the only thing that damns us and keeps us from eternal life is unforgiven sin. Satan can tempt us, taunt us, and mock us with sin, but he cannot damn us. When Christ died for our sins and rose again, He took away the only thing that separates us from God—unforgiven sin. His resurrection proves that He *is* life, and it proves the genuineness of the eternal life He offers us if we come to Him for salvation.

And once we conclude that in Jesus' eyes death is not primarily physical, then we also can conclude that life is not primarily physical. Resurrection to new life is not just a physical transaction. There's a spiritual transaction that takes place, giving new life to the believer. And the power that raised Christ from the dead is the exact same power *we* experience as we walk in Christ, the giver of eternal life.

As the apostle Paul tells us, "If we have been united together in the likeness of His death, certainly we also shall be in the likeness of His resurrection" (Romans 6:5).

That is the essence of salvation—new life in Christ Jesus.

CHAPTER 5

THE REALITY OF ETERNITY: HE IS ALIVE

*Do not be afraid; I am the First and the Last. I am
He who lives, and was dead, and behold, I am alive
forevermore. Amen. And I have the keys of Hades
and of Death.*

—REVELATION 1:17–18

The cathedral in Milan, Italy, is the second largest Gothic
cathedral in the world. On the arches above a triple door-
way are three inscriptions. The one on the right reads, "All that
pleases is but for a moment." The inscription on the left reads, "All
that troubles is but for a moment." And above the central door are
these words: "Nothing is important save that which is eternal."

This may sound obvious, but eternity is forever! Life on earth
is temporary at best, but eternity awaits us all. Tragically, many

people here rarely think of eternity, much less prepare for it. Nevertheless, whether or not we're prepared, all human beings will face it and will realize the consequences of their preparation.

KNOW THE TRUTH

There was a teacher who got caught up in a business scheme in which she invested her entire life savings. She was new to such investments but was talked into it by a smooth-tongued broker who promised certain riches. When the deal fell apart and the woman lost all her money, she contacted the Better Business Bureau. It didn't take them long to help her see that it was all a scam from the very beginning.

They asked the woman, "Why didn't you come to us earlier? Why didn't you seek our advice?"

She dropped her head and replied, "I thought about it. But I was afraid you would tell me not to do it." The cost for her reluctance to hear the truth was her life savings.

Many people don't want to hear the truth about God, and so they don't try to find out. But it will cost them eternal life.

Many don't want to hear the truth about God, so they don't try to find out.

The Bible is telling the truth about Jesus being the only way to eternal life. "There is one God and one Mediator between God and men, the Man Christ Jesus" (1 Timothy

2:5). Why is Jesus the only one through whom we can go to heaven? Because of *the resurrection.*

The resurrection of Jesus is unique among all religions in the world. Every religious leader who has ever walked this earth has died and is still dead to this day. Jesus alone has been resurrected from the dead—not resuscitated back to life, but resurrected into new life.

If Jesus had not been raised, He would be nothing more than any other good religious teacher to come along before or since. In fact, as Paul tells us, "If Christ is not risen, your faith is futile; you are still in your sins!" (1 Corinthians 15:17).

JESUS IS TRUTH

Remember again that Jesus came *from eternity.* He stepped into time and space and lived on this earth to communicate the truth about eternal life and to provide our safe passage into it. His perspective on life and death is much different than ours—and He's telling the truth. He tells us, "Do not be afraid," then proclaims, "I am the First and the Last. I am He who lives, and was dead, and behold, I am alive forevermore. Amen. And I have the keys of Hades and of Death" (Revelation 1:17–18).

We've already described how Jesus defined life and death. But let's hear it again: what we call "death" is to Christ not death at all—it is sleep. And He didn't come to save us from sleep, but to deliver us from death. We will all sleep, saints and sinners alike—but we will not all die!

That's why the most important thing about Christ's death and resurrection was not physical but spiritual. He both slept and died. He was physically dead, and He was spiritually dead. For the wages of sin is *death*—spiritual separation from the heavenly Father.

The most important thing about Christ's death and resurrection was not physical but spiritual.

Once the price for sin was paid in full through the death of Christ, the heavenly Father raised Him from the dead—physically and spiritually. It was not resuscitation, but resurrection. He conquered sin and death, and His resurrection is proof positive.

Jesus was telling the truth when He said, "I am the resurrection and the life. He who believes in Me, though he may die, he shall live. And whoever lives and believes in Me shall never die" (John 11:25–26). He went from heaven to this world, then to the grave, then back into this world, then to heaven. So He *knows* what He's talking about.

Because of Christ, the grave is not the end for us; it is not to be feared. His resurrection demonstrated that beyond physical death is a place more wonderful than we can imagine, in the presence of God.

When Jesus said we would have abundant life, He was talking

about *eternal life*. Because He lives, we too shall live. Resurrection is a state in which believers *enjoy* their eternal destiny—a life beyond this life.

ETERNAL LIFE

The resurrection is the clearest evidence that eternity is real and that everything must be seen against the backdrop of eternity. Jesus said on many occasions that those who believe in Him would never die. Yet believers "die" all the time; that is, their physical bodies die and are given back to the ground. If Jesus' priority was life on earth, He would have abolished our physical death. But that isn't what Jesus did, for that wasn't His priority. Eternity was His focus. Living forever was what the resurrection accomplished.

Concerning what Jesus accomplished through His cross and resurrection, the Bible says that "having been perfected, He became the author of eternal salvation to all who obey Him" (Hebrews 5:9). Jesus came from eternity, and He will bring all those who believe in Him to eternity. The resurrection demonstrated that death could not hold Him in the grave, nor did it have power over Him. And because He is eternal, this eternal nature is given to all who are in Christ.

His promise is striking: "Whoever lives and believes in Me shall never die" (John 11:26). The resurrection was not for earthly salvation, but *eternal salvation.*

ETERNAL DEATH

Take careful note that the promised power of the resurrection applies only to those who obey Him. Eternity awaits everybody, but new life is only for those who obey.

The writer of Hebrews mentions the doctrine of "eternal *judgment*" (6:2). Yes, eternity awaits all people. Some will enjoy eternal life, while others must endure eternal death.

Jesus often talked about the reality of eternity for believers and nonbelievers alike. In Matthew 25:31–46, Jesus gave a long description of how the "Son of Man" will judge all the nations. He'll sort out everyone as a shepherd divides sheep from goats. To some He will say, "Come, you blessed of My Father, inherit the kingdom prepared for you from the foundation of the world" (verse 34). To others He'll say, "Depart from Me, you cursed, into the everlasting fire prepared for the devil and his angels" (verse 41).

His last statement in this passage reflects His understanding of eternity: "And these will go away into everlasting punishment, but the righteous into eternal life" (verse 46).

ETERNAL KINGDOMS

The Bible talks of two kingdoms in this world—the kingdom of God and the kingdom of Satan. One is the kingdom of light, the other the kingdom of darkness.

Evil is a reality. It exists apart from you and me, and apart from our individual actions. Long before we were born, sin was in the world. As Paul explained, "For we do not wrestle against flesh and blood, but against principalities, against powers, against the rulers of the darkness of this age, against the spiritual hosts of wickedness in the heavenly places" (Ephesians 6:12). Evil is a great power at work, a great kingdom fighting for supremacy over all our lives.

In Scripture, the "kingdom of darkness" or "walking in darkness" represents all that is opposed to God and His purpose for your life. Walking in darkness means you live in such a way that you rarely have any thought about God at all, or if you do think about Him, you don't think of Him as "light and in Him is no darkness at all" (1 John 1:5). You think of Him more as some tender father figure who's ready to smile upon your failures, who will pat you on the head, and who, on the basis of your goodness and His, will grant you entry into heaven someday when you die. That is walking in darkness.

So many fail to realize that the very nature of mankind is sinful, opposed to God in every way.

So many people don't understand what God is really like. They don't understand their own condition against the backdrop of eternity. They fail to realize that the very nature of mankind is sinful, opposed to God in every way. But we have only to look at the cross to know that God takes sin seriously and will not allow it into a perfect place called heaven.

There's an incredible distance between God and sinful mankind. How far is it between light and dark? They aren't even in the same room. If there's any light there at all, then it isn't dark. Likewise, to live in the state of sin means that you're completely removed from the God of light—and desperately in need of a Savior.

Eternity is real, hence the need for resurrection. Jesus therefore is the key to eternal life. He's the One who died for our sins and then rose victorious over sin and death.

Listen again to these words from our resurrected Lord: "Do not be afraid; I am the First and the Last. I am He who lives, and was dead, and behold, I am alive forevermore. Amen. And I have the keys of Hades and of Death" (Revelation 1:17–18). He's "alive forevermore"—what a wonderful statement! That's the hope we have in Jesus Christ.

SPIRITUAL REUNIONS

One of the great men in our family, Melvin Wells Sr., recently passed from this life. He was a dedicated Christian deacon, he was involved in church planting, and he took an early retirement from his business to go as a missionary to Africa. He lived a godly life that inspired all of us who come after him.

According to Jesus' perspective, did this man die? No, he sleeps. Melvin Wells Sr. put his faith in Jesus Christ, and he *cannot* see death. The resurrection has saved him from death and given him new life in Christ.

Another godly man in our family was Gerald Sanders Blackaby. He too followed the risen Lord throughout his life. He was a businessman on a mission with God. Though his career was banking, he started churches in every town where he was posted. As a layperson, he taught himself Greek so he could preach with deeper understanding. He stood for what was right in town hall meetings and passed on a rich heritage of faith to the family. Did he die? Of course not. He's alive in the presence of the resurrected Christ. His physical body is in the ground, but his spirit lives forever in eternity.

Because of the resurrection, we can have confidence that we'll have a spiritual family reunion someday.

Why can we have confidence that we'll have a spiritual family reunion someday? *Because of the resurrection*— which has eternity written all over it. Why else would Jesus come to earth and die for our sin? Why would He rise to new life and come back to encourage His followers?

The Father loves us and has provided a way for eternal salvation. Nothing else in life really matters except to secure our eternal destiny.

ETERNAL PRIORITIES

When Jesus sent out seventy of His followers to preach and prepare the way for Him to visit various cities (Luke 10:1–20), He made sure they kept eternity in their sights. They were to proclaim, "The kingdom of God has come near to you" (verse 9).

When they returned from this mission, they reported amazing success and miracles through their hands. Having gone out in the power of Jesus' name, they witnessed the impossible. Even demons fell subject to their authority (verse 17).

This successful ministry report was encouraging, but Jesus kept it in proper perspective. He told these men:

> I saw Satan fall like lightning from heaven. Behold,
> I give you the authority to trample on serpents and
> scorpions, and over all the power of the enemy, and
> nothing shall by any means hurt you. Nevertheless do
> not rejoice in this, that the spirits are subject to you,
> but rather rejoice because your names are written in
> heaven. (verses 18–20)

His words are a strong reminder: Don't be distracted by success. Don't find your joy in accomplishments. Don't find your identity in the things you do or the job you have.

Instead, rejoice in this and this alone: *your names are written in heaven!* Rejoice in the fact that God has chosen you, that God has blessed you, that God is working through you. Your great joy is found in your relationship to God, who has made a way for you to enjoy eternity with Him. And through your life, He's working to bring others to eternal life through the gospel of Jesus Christ.

We should never get distracted by good works or a successful ministry, but simply be thankful for our salvation. We should be endlessly grateful that we're saved from sin and born into the family of God, especially with the knowledge of what it cost to provide eternal life.

Being a Christian does not mean trying to live a good life, trying to be better than everyone else, striving to perform certain church rituals, or believing the right doctrines. It means a relationship with the risen Lord. It means living the new life He provided through the resurrection. That reality impacts every area of our lives. It sets new priorities and submits the temporal to the eternal.

Resurrection changes everything. It changes the way we raise our children, for now we realize that their souls are eternal. It changes the way we invest our money, for all material things will be burned up, and only that which is eternal will last. It changes the way we use our time, for time on earth is short, while eternity is forever. It changes the way we see people, for no matter how evil they may appear, we don't want to see anybody sent to eternal judgment.

The primary concern of Jesus was to secure our souls for eternal life.

What is the priority of your life?

PART THREE

The Resurrection in the Believer's Experience

CHAPTER 6

RESURRECTION LIFE

*That I may know Him and the power of His
resurrection, and the fellowship of His sufferings,
being conformed to His death, if, by any means, I
may attain to the resurrection from the dead.*
—PHILIPPIANS 3:10–11

The cross and the resurrection began in the heart of God. They were lived out in the life of Jesus Christ, God's Son.

But their full impact hits *our* lives: *we* are the reason the Father sent His Son. The cross and resurrection were not for the sake of Jesus, but for our sakes.

And as a result of what the Father has done, the resurrection is something believers can experience in daily life…as well as something we'll experience for all eternity.

FEAR AND GREAT JOY

Let's take a moment to read through Matthew's account of that pivotal day in human history, the day Jesus rose from the dead:

> Now after the Sabbath, as the first day of the week began
> to dawn, Mary Magdalene and the other Mary came to
> see the tomb. And behold, there was a great earthquake;
> for an angel of the Lord descended from heaven, and
> came and rolled back the stone from the door, and sat on
> it. His countenance was like lightning, and his clothing as
> white as snow. And the guards shook for fear of him, and
> became like dead men. But the angel answered and said to
> the women, "Do not be afraid, for I know that you seek
> Jesus who was crucified. He is not here; for He is risen, as
> He said. Come, see the place where the Lord lay. And go
> quickly and tell His disciples that He is risen from the
> dead, and indeed He is going before you into Galilee;
> there you will see Him. Behold, I have told you." So they
> went out quickly from the tomb with fear and great joy,
> and ran to bring His disciples word. (Matthew 28:1–8)

The power of the resurrection was dramatic. It came with "a great earthquake" and an angel "like lightning…as white as snow." The massive stone that sealed the entrance was casually moved aside and used as a resting place for the angel who sat upon it. Seasoned Roman soldiers were overcome with fear and fainted as "dead men."

This resurrection power was not of this world. It was beyond the scope of any earthly experience. The world demonstrates power by taking life, but God demonstrates His power by giving it. How much power do you think it takes to bring life into that which was dead? Well, that same power is what God has provided to set you free from sin and its deadly consequences.

The world demonstrates power by taking life; God demonstrates His power by giving it.

And just as the women responded to the resurrection with "fear and great joy," so we are overwhelmed at its prospects. New life always brings great joy, but the power of the resurrection also instills a sense of fear. We realize very quickly that this is outside our scope of experience. It's not something we control; rather, it controls us. The divine has interacted with the mortal. Eternity has crossed into time.

We have no prior reference point for the resurrection. It's uniquely a divine act of God.

DEATH PRECEDES RESURRECTION

Resurrection is the power of God to give new life. It's the power to bring you into the holy of holies, the place of direct and personal contact with the living God.

This resurrection power is available to all human beings—with only one condition: *you must die.* The power of the resurrection is found in the ability to die. Resurrection power is on the other side of a conscious decision to die to self and give your life to Christ. It requires a decision of the will to be crucified with Christ, that the Father might raise you to new life.

Are you starting to understand that we aren't talking about physical death? All people will physically die, but not all people will be resurrected to new life—for this "new life" begins the moment you accept Jesus Christ as your Lord and Savior. Physical death is just the moment that reveals who has received this new life and who remains in death. Physical death pulls back the curtain and reveals the condition of our souls. It reveals whether we've been born again—whether the resurrected Christ has come into our lives and given us eternal life.

CRUCIFIED WITH CHRIST

Many Christians look at the cross and accept the fact that Jesus was the only true sacrifice for our sins. They reflect upon that great event and say, "Christ died for me, a sinner. I'm so grateful He took my place on the cross." And while that's true—that only the perfect Son of God could satisfy the requirement of taking our sins on the cross—it doesn't mean we don't go to the cross ourselves.

Paul wrote, "I have been crucified with Christ; it is no longer I who live, but Christ lives in me" (Galatians 2:20). He went beyond saying that someone was crucified in his place. Paul said *he* had been crucified *with* Christ.

It's difficult for us to fully comprehend what Paul was saying. In some sense, he experienced a touch of what Christ endured on that cross. Somehow, in Paul's life, he lingered long enough at the foot of the cross that he began to experience within himself the pain and agony that Christ felt. Christ had endured this pain and agony on Paul's behalf, and Paul internalized this experience. And as a result, he would never again be the same.

Christ's death literally caused Paul to die to self and live to Christ. He understood the depths of what sin had done to the Lord, and in his spirit, Paul went to the cross and died with Him. He took the time at the cross to understand that event very intimately—so much so that he could say, "I have been crucified with Christ; it is no longer I who live, but Christ lives in me."

In our lives, there must also come a point when we can truly say, "I have been crucified with Christ."

VICTORY IS IN CHRIST

For some, this is moving into an area that's very foreign to their thinking. Others can smile, for they know exactly what we're talking about here. But let us say it again: the secret to resurrection power is that you must die before you can be resurrected. Your sin must be dealt with. Just as Jesus taught, if you try to save your life, you'll lose it. But if you lose your life for His sake, you'll find it.

Think back to Jesus' life. Did He resurrect Himself? No, the Father raised Him up. What part did Jesus play? *He died.* He obeyed the Father unto death.

What part did Jesus play in the resurrection? He died. He obeyed the Father unto death.

Likewise, the power of the resurrection is what the Father does in you when you die to self and choose to live in Christ. *You die; the Father resurrects.*

He does not resurrect you to a better life, but to a new life. The apostle Paul experienced this new life in Christ, which he described this way:

> For the love of Christ compels us, because we judge thus:
> that if One died for all, then all died; and He died for all,
> that those who live should live no longer for themselves,
> but for Him who died for them and rose again…. There-
> fore, if anyone is in Christ, he is a new creation; old
> things have passed away; behold, all things have become
> new. (2 Corinthians 5:14–15, 17)

Jesus died for us—that we might live for Him. Apart from Him, we're left in our sin and remain in a state of separation from

God. Hear this carefully: Physically, we're born and live until we die; *we progress toward physical death.* Spiritually, we're dead until we're made alive in Christ; *we progress toward eternal life.*

So the kingdom of God is exactly the opposite of the kingdom of the world. We're hopelessly dead in sin until we're granted new life in Christ through the power of His resurrection. Paul described it this way:

> But God, who is rich in mercy, because of His great love with which He loved us, even when we were dead in trespasses, made us alive together with Christ (by grace you have been saved), and raised us up together, and made us sit together in the heavenly places in Christ Jesus. (Ephesians 2:4–6)

RESTORED RELATIONSHIP

Our sin has left us separated from God. Left to ourselves, we're spiritually dead and cannot know Him. That sin, if it isn't removed, will destroy us eternally. We cannot know abundant life as God intended. For unless we die to self, our sin will inevitably break our relationship with a holy God.

I (Mel) had a challenging stretch in high school, when I was testing the waters. As a result, I was called into the office to have a meeting with the vice principal. Apparently, I'd missed a lot of classes, even though it wasn't long into the school year. No, I hadn't been sick—I just had better things to do. It's not that I was doing a lot of terrible things. I was just more interested in fun than in attending classes. The vice principal and I had a good lit-

Unless we die to self, our sin inevitably breaks our relationship with a holy God.

tle heart-to-heart talk, and he made it very clear that I was wrong and he was right.

Later that day I had a soccer game. Dad happened to show up to support

his son. Unfortunately, the vice principal was also a soccer fan and was standing on the sidelines when Dad arrived. They knew each other, and they talked for what seemed like the entire game. I just knew I'd been ratted out, and Dad was now aware of the trouble I was in.

When Dad offered to give me a ride home after the game, I avoided him. "No thanks, I'll walk home with my friends." Believe me, I took my time about it.

When I arrived home, I was afraid to go in the door. I was sure Dad would drop the hammer. So I quietly slipped into my room without him noticing I was there.

Then it happened. I heard him call out, "Mel!" I just knew he'd talked with Mom, they'd mapped out the game plan for my punishment and were ready to hit me with the bad news. I heard him again: "Mel…time for supper!" That's all.

So I joined the family for supper, but nothing tasted good. I couldn't eat. I was a wreck.

After supper, I went back to my room and anxiously awaited the confrontation. But it never came. In fact, to this day, I don't know if Dad ever found out about my talk with the vice principal.

My relationship with Dad was strained, and yet Dad had not done a thing to cause it. I was experiencing the result of my own actions, and it was eating me up. Had my dad changed? No. Had my home changed? No. Had my heart changed? Yes! I was feeling the weight of my sin. As a result, I had a strained relationship with my parents.

The same is true in our relationship with the heavenly Father. Our sin creates a separation; it damages the relationship. But *He* has not changed—it's only the result of our sin.

What you're experiencing in life is the sum total of choices you've made with God. You've been given the choice to make Jesus Christ the Lord of your life. And He is able to remove your sin and provide safe passage into eternity, where you'll enjoy a perfect relationship with your heavenly Father.

HE WILL GUIDE YOU

There's a story of a Muslim in Africa who became a Christian. Some of his friends asked, "Why have you become a Christian?"

He answered, "Well, it's like this. Suppose you were going down the road, and suddenly the road forked in two directions, and you didn't know which way to go. There at the fork were two men, one dead and one alive—who would you ask which way to go?"

Jesus is alive—and we can trust Him to lead us to eternity with His Father. The resurrection is proof that He knows what He's talking about.

Jesus is alive—and we can trust Him to lead us to eternity with His Father.

Recall again that when the Bible speaks of resurrection as applied to our lives, it's nearly always talking about the power for overcoming sin. There's so much more to the resurrection than going to heaven when you die. In fact, the power of the resurrection is primarily strength for today. It gives victory over sin and tears down the wall separating us from God. It frees us from the dominion of darkness and brings us into the kingdom of light. It provides a relationship with the risen Christ, who loves us and gave His life for us. It's what opens the door to all God has promised to those who put their trust in Him.

There's so much more to life—and it's found in the death and resurrection of Jesus Christ.

Death and resurrection go together; dying to self and living with Christ cannot be separated. Paul described what this meant personally for him in these words:

> But what things were gain to me, these I have counted loss for Christ. Yet indeed I also count all things loss for the excellence of the knowledge of Christ Jesus my Lord,

for whom I have suffered the loss of all things, and count
them as rubbish, that I may gain Christ and be found in
Him, not having my own righteousness, which is from
the law, but that which is through faith in Christ, the
righteousness which is from God by faith; that I may
know Him and the power of His resurrection, and the fellowship of His sufferings, being conformed to His death,
if, by any means, I may attain to the resurrection from the
dead. (Philippians 3:7–10)

It was Paul's sincere desire to know Christ experientially. He
wanted to experience intimately both the power of His resurrection and the fellowship of His sufferings—and they both go hand
in hand. Paul so desired to experience resurrection power that he
was willing to be conformed to Christ's death.

IT COSTS SOMETHING

We enjoy flying, but those overseas trips can be tough on the
body. A trip to do mission work in Africa takes its toll, but it's well
worth the benefit.

But suppose someone said, "I would love to experience a mission trip to Africa, but I won't fly. I *really* want to go…but I just
can't. The trip would be too demanding." If this was their attitude,
they would never experience Africa, however much they wanted

to, because it's not practical to get to Africa without flying. They would have to settle for photographs, stories, and dreams of what could have been. But they would never step foot in Africa or understand its beauty.

We often hear people say, "I want to experience the power of the resurrection with all my heart." Then we watch their lives—and they won't board the plane to cross over the ocean.

The distance between a life that's experiencing the power of the resurrected Christ and a life without Christ is vast. And you cannot reach the resurrected life without first going through the cross. People want resurrection without suffering; they want resurrection without death. But that is impossible.

Before Jesus was resurrected, He had to die. He had to go to Jerusalem, where He would be arrested, beaten, whipped, forced to wear a crown of thorns, publicly humiliated, and nailed to a cross. All of that happened before the resurrection.

Without the cross there is no resurrection. They go hand in hand. Hear again these words from Paul:

> We were buried with Him through baptism into death,
> that just as Christ was raised from the dead by the glory
> of the Father, even so we also should walk in newness of
> life. For if we have been united together in the likeness of
> His death, certainly we also shall be in the likeness of His
> resurrection. (Romans 6:4–5)

Do you see the connection? Those who are buried with Him will rise with Him, those united in His death will be united in His resurrection, those crucified will have victory over sin—just like Him.

We want you to realize that resurrection power is something you can *know;* newness of life is something you can *experience*—if you so choose. But Jesus said, "If anyone desires to come after Me, let him deny himself, and take up his cross, and follow Me" (Matthew 16:24).

Resurrection power is something you can know— if you so choose.

THREE ESSENTIAL QUESTIONS

So let us ask you three simple questions.

First, do you *want* resurrection life? Do you really want to know the power of the resurrection and the life God created you to know?

We ask this question because many don't want it. Oh, they may say they do, but their lives contradict what they say.

Did you sense the tone in Paul's voice as he longed to know Christ and the power of the resurrection? This was more important to him than anything in the world—more important than money, fame, or worldly pleasure.

After Paul met the risen Lord, he desired life with Christ more than life itself. The question is simple: Do *you* also have this desire? Do you truly want His power in your life?

We're convinced that most people do *not* want it. They want to go to heaven when they die, but they don't want His power on earth. For with the power comes responsibility; with the power comes accountability. There's an expectation that you have to act godly—and who wants that? There's the obligation to live like Jesus—not just in His resurrection but in His cross.

There are many who don't want to die to self and allow Christ to live in them because they don't want to give up all their sin. They like their sin too much. They know they'll have to forgive someone, and they don't want to. They'll need to put Him first in their finances and tithe, and they would rather spend their money on themselves. They'll be compelled to honor the Sabbath and be faithful in church, and they don't want to give up their weekends. They know they'll have to serve others, and they'd rather not get involved. They know they'll need to publicly confess Him, and they'd prefer to remain quiet. They want to know the risen Lord— but they don't want Him too involved in their life.

But hear it again: the secret to resurrection power is that you have to die before you can be resurrected. Jesus said that if you try to save your life, you will lose it, but if you lose your life for His sake, you will find it.

You can't effectively get to Africa without getting on a plane; you can't experience resurrection without dying to self. The power of the resurrection is on the other side of a conscious decision to give your life to Christ. It's a decision of the will to be crucified with Christ, that the Father might raise you to new life. *Do you want resurrection life?*

Our second question is this: Are you *pursuing* resurrection life? If you say you want resurrection life, does your life demonstrate that desire? Would others conclude that you want to know Christ and the power of His resurrection because of how much time you spend in prayer? and in His Word? and with His people? and in worship? From watching the way you live your life, would others conclude that you want to know the Lord more than anything in the world?

> *If you say you want resurrection life, does your life demonstrate that desire?*

Would we know you're walking with Christ by how you make decisions in life, because you've been reoriented to eternal priorities? Do you consult Him when you make your plans? Have you chosen to give Him first place in your schedule?

Would we know that Christ is your all in all by your conversations? Do you love to hear stories of what He's doing in other people's lives? Do you ask others what He's doing? Do you share with others what He's doing in you?

When it comes right down to it, are you willing to risk seeking after the Lord, knowing that it might change your life? You realize that when He speaks, things change—and you want to hear Him anyway. Let's be honest—an encounter with the risen Christ is life changing. *Are you pursuing resurrection life?*

Third question: What is your *decision*? Will you give your life completely to Christ, that you might know the power of the resurrection and the fellowship of His sufferings?

If there's a hesitation to answer that question, don't expect to experience Him in your life. For He is not yet Lord. You may want Him to be Lord, but you aren't willing to go to the cross and die.

We're primarily talking here not to those who are still unbelievers, but to those who call themselves Christians. Deep down in your soul, do you hear the call of God wanting more of you?

Deep in your soul, do you hear the call of God wanting more of you?

As we come to worship and hear the voice of God, we're told, "Do not harden your hearts" (Psalm 95:8). Don't walk away without responding to the One who called you by name. That could be fatal.

So what's your decision?

PROCLAIMING LIBERTY TO THE CAPTIVE

We have to admit that when we look at some Christians' lives, we want to say, "Surely you can't be satisfied with that! You really don't have to be miserable. You don't have to hold on to that bitterness. You don't have to withdraw from God's people and be critical of them. Instead, you can know the joy of the Lord, find passion in life, and know the power of the resurrection. You can make a difference with your life that will last for eternity!"

One day Jesus entered the synagogue in Nazareth and read from Isaiah 61:

The Spirit of the LORD is upon Me,
Because He has anointed Me
To preach the gospel to the poor;
He has sent Me to heal the
    brokenhearted,
To proclaim liberty to the captives
And recovery of sight to the blind,
To set at liberty those who are
    oppressed;
To proclaim the acceptable year of the
    LORD. (Luke 4:18–19)

He is fulfilling this calling still today. Jesus provides freedom from the power of sin and new life in Him.

It seems like an easy choice to make, yet many remain spiritually dead and miss out on life. They're unwilling to let go and obey the Lord. They're unwilling to die that they may find life. They're unwilling to humble themselves so God can lift them up.

The Lord says, "Stop eying the reward—keep your eyes on Me. It is not just heaven someday; it is life today. Make a choice to receive Me...all of Me. Take My life, death, and resurrection."

What will it look like for you to live in the power of the resurrection? Can you say right now that you are experiencing new life in Christ as God intended? Do you believe you're expressing that power adequately to your family, your church, and the world?

If not, you need to die to self and allow Him to live in you. It's a choice!

CHAPTER 7

RESURRECTION AND THE UNCOMMON LIFE

Peter answered Him and said, "Lord, if it is You, command me to come to You on the water." So He said, "Come."

—MATTHEW 14:28–29

Have you watched other people accomplish a remarkable task, yet it appeared to you to be quite easy? Though what they did may have even been amazing, you still thought, *I could do that.*

As the saying goes, easier said than done.

When we read of people in the Bible, we tend to pick them apart for how they failed. We notice their lack of faith, we marvel at their weaknesses, and we're baffled at why they didn't listen better to God. We tell ourselves, *If I was there, I would have obeyed. I wouldn't have doubted.* Especially concerning the disciples in the gospels, we imagine, *If only I'd had the opportunity to walk with Jesus like those guys did, I could have been part of amazing things.*

The characters in the Bible were ordinary people—faced with extraordinary situations. They had to choose to walk by faith or to walk by sight. Those who chose to walk by faith experienced the mighty power of God working in their lives. They got to live an uncommon life with an extraordinary God.

If you want to live in such a way as to experience the resurrection, you'll find yourself in the middle of impossible situations.

If you want to experience the resurrection, you'll find yourself in impossible situations.

The resurrection itself is impossible—it's in the realm of the divine and beyond anything you can do in your own strength. It is God-sized in nature. As you experience it, don't be surprised if God takes you into things that are impossible for the average human being. Resurrection life brings uncommon experiences and takes you where you never would have gone otherwise. And it challenges your faith to its furthest limit.

EXPLORING NEW TERRITORY

If you're asking God to let you experience the resurrection, you're asking Him to take you into a place you've never been. So don't complain when He does.

God never does things the way we think they should be

done. His ways are not our ways; His thoughts are not our thoughts. That's why faith is required to follow Him. Faith is fundamental to the resurrection life as God leads us into impossible situations. He takes us to the end of ourselves—and beyond.

It has always been that way. In both Old and New Testaments, people were taken beyond themselves to a place where only God could bring the victory, and we see what only He could do. That is the realm of the divine; that is where the risen Christ lives. And you can anticipate the same challenge in your life.

Resurrection life is about walking with God. Every time a person moves into that arena of divine life, miracles happen. This is true in the Old Testament, in the New Testament, and today.

MOSES AND A DEAD END

When you examine the great leaders in the Bible, the life of the divine in human flesh is obvious.

Moses was called upon to lead the Israelites out of Egypt, where they'd been slaves for many years. God told Moses, "I will send you to Pharaoh that you may bring My people...out of Egypt" (Exodus 3:10). When Pharaoh resisted and a host of plagues came upon the land, God's power was displayed. Finally, Pharaoh gave in and the people of God escaped. They left the country with all the wealth of the land. Then Pharaoh had a change of heart and sent an army to recover them.

As the people fled, they came to the Red Sea—they were trapped with nowhere to go. They looked back and saw the Egyptian army bearing down on them. The sound of the hoofbeats of their chariot horses grew louder.

Here was Moses with a nation of people who were trapped, unarmed, and bewildered. And an angry army was about to wipe them out.

In that situation, you would probably be thinking, *God, why did You bring us out of Egypt to die here? We have nowhere to go! There's no hope of escape!* But was that true? Was there *nowhere* to turn? Had they come that far for nothing?

No, God parted the Red Sea, the people walked across on dry land, and the entire Egyptian army was wiped out when the water swept down upon them.

After taking Moses and the Israelites into a place of absolutely no escape, God then proceeded to lead them into the Promised Land in a way that only He could have done. And the world marveled at the mighty power of God.

JOSHUA AND A RIDICULOUS PLAN

Consider Joshua, who set out to lead the people of Israel against the heavily fortified city of Jericho. He had just taken over leadership of the people from Moses and was about to enter the Promised Land. Before they crossed the Jordan River, he sent in spies to check out the warrior-filled city so they could draw up a battle plan.

But what was God's battle plan? He told them the men were to march around the city once for six days, then seven times on the seventh day. They would blow their trumpets. Seven priests would carry seven rams' horns before the ark of the covenant. On Joshua's command, all the people would shout at the top of their lungs. And, by the way, the only people in Jericho that God would spare would be a harlot, Rahab, and her family.

If you were Joshua, what would you be thinking? *Lord, I'm not sure I heard You right. The trumpets were playing so loud, and I must have misunderstood You.* No, Joshua heard right.

And again, the Lord gave the victory. Not one Israelite soldier was lost. And the world feared the power of the Israelites' God.

GIDEON AND IMPOSSIBLE ODDS

Gideon was another man called to lead the Israelites against a fierce army. He was not a warrior. In fact, he was afraid of the enemy. But God told him to lead the people into battle against an enemy that numbered one hundred twenty thousand men in arms.

Gideon established an army of thirty-two thousand men. God told him, "That's too many men. Tell whoever is afraid to go home." Apparently Gideon wasn't the only one intimidated by the enemy, for twenty-two thousand men accepted that offer.

Gideon was left with an army of only ten thousand. God said again, "Too many men. Whoever drinks from the water on his knees, let him go home." And wouldn't you know it? Kneeling by the stream was the preferred method of drinking water among warriors. And now Gideon had only three hundred men left.

He may have thought (as many of us might think), *What am I doing here? This battle is hopeless! We're going to get killed!* But was that true? No, Gideon's three hundred men defeated an army of one hundred and twenty thousand. Once again, not one Israelite was lost in battle.

God had taken Gideon and Israel into a no-win situation—and destroyed the enemy with a resounding victory. And the world saw God's hand of protection over His people.

That's how God works: taking people into impossible situations, then displaying His power in their midst.

Time after time, God took people into impossible situations and then displayed His power in their midst. *That's how God works.*

PETER AND THE ABSURD

Let's look at another significant moment, this time in the New Testament. In Matthew 14:22–33, we find Peter and the other disciples in a boat on the Sea of Galilee during a storm. They're there because Jesus had earlier commanded them to get into that boat and cross to the other side.

It was now the middle of the night, and their lives were in danger. The waves grew higher, the wind was blowing stronger, and water began filling the boat.

Imagine what might have gone through the minds of the disciples. *Why did we listen to Jesus? He's only a carpenter, and we're fishermen. We should have known better than to be out in a storm like this.*

Scripture is very clear on this point: "Jesus *made* His disciples get into the boat and go before Him" (14:22). Jesus put them into danger—and didn't even go with them! Well, that's only half true. Jesus did come to them a bit later—*walking on the water.*

When the disciples saw a figure of a man out on the water, they were terrified and thought for sure it was a ghost. There was no other explanation. After all, flesh-and-blood people don't walk on water.

Jesus knew their fear, and He told them, "Be of good cheer! It is I; do not be afraid." Immediately Peter responded with great courage: "Lord, if it is You, command me to come to You on the water." Then comes this amazing statement. "And when Peter had come down out of the boat, *he walked on the water* to go to Jesus" (verses 27–29). Talk about the uncommon life! Nobody had ever walked on water, before or since this moment. Jesus had called Peter to come to Him on the water. Peter obeyed, and he experienced a miracle.

Remember, Peter wasn't alone in that boat. All the other disciples were right there watching this scene unfold before them. But they remained in the boat while Peter was out with Jesus walking on the waves. He may have been a little crazy, but you have to admire his courage.

Maybe some of the other disciples were thinking, *I could do that!* No, they couldn't. What Peter did takes *faith*—and their human reasoning wouldn't even let them get out of the boat. Likewise, when Peter went back to human reasoning, he got into trouble at once. Taking his eyes off Jesus, he glanced at the storm and thought, *What have I done?* He saw the waves and began to doubt—and to sink.

But don't you admire Peter? At least he had the courage to try! He loved Jesus and desperately wanted to be with Him. Surely Jesus was proud of Peter, as He reached out and grabbed Peter's hand to rescue him.

At that moment, Jesus said to Peter, "O you of little faith, why did you doubt?" (verse 31). Reading those words, what tone do you sense in Jesus' voice? Frustration? Harshness? The more we study this passage, the more likely it seems that Jesus spoke those words with a tone of encouragement. He knew that the thought of walking on water was absolutely absurd to the human mind. As He spoke to Peter, it must have been with a grin on his face. "Peter, you already made it so far! You were already walking on water. Why did you start to doubt?" Peter still had a ways to go, but he was growing in faith right before his Lord's eyes. Everyone else was still in the boat, but Peter was living life on the edge. He was learning more each day about the uncommon life of a disciple.

GOD AND THE IMPOSSIBLE

Have you been in that place? that place where Jesus takes you? that place of no return?

You took a step of faith and started on the journey, but circumstances now seem impossible. You *Have you been where Jesus takes you, the place of no return?* began examining your position and got scared. You've started to question God's call. You can't go back, but it also seems you can't go forward. All you know to do is to cry out to God.

Be assured: *you're in a good place.* You may be where God has been leading you all along. He had to get you where you are now so He can show you more of Himself than you've ever known.

So don't quit. Don't hesitate. Don't turn back. Simply call out His name. Depend on Him! For He has you right where He wants you.

It's just like God to bring you to helplessness so you'll cry out to Him and find His provision. And in that place He does what

He's planned to do all along. He parts the Red Sea, He conquers Jericho, He defeats the enemy, He saves a sinking Peter. *He meets every need that He created.*

Have you heard the phrase "It's my way or the highway"? When it comes to God, His way *is* the "high" way. He moves on a plane much higher than we do. He doesn't function within our limitations. He isn't restricted by nature's laws; He made nature. He is God!

And following His ways, with Him in full control, is resurrection life at its best.

Don't always assume that a difficult situation is a result of some mistake you made. Perhaps God brought you to this difficult situation so you might see His mighty power.

One of the ways God teaches you to trust Him is to place you in a church that's walking by faith. It's a great place to be, walking together with other believers who are following after Christ. We can pray for one another, encourage one another, walk with one another, and give one another strength when we face the impossible.

Think back to Peter on the water that wonderful night. Why did Jesus have Peter come to Him on the water? So Peter could brag to his friends? No, it was because He was shaping the character of Peter to be a great leader in the early church. The early Christians would need a spiritual leader who knew Christ and would walk by faith. Peter would prove to be such a man, full of faith and confident in Christ.

It was Peter who preached the first gospel sermon on the Day of Pentecost, when three thousand souls were saved and baptized into the church (Acts 2:14–41). It was Peter who healed a man lame since birth (3:1–8), who defied the religious elite in Jerusalem (4:5–20), who raised the dead to life (9:36–41), who took the gospel to the Gentile centurion Cornelius (10:24–48), who was freed from prison by an angel of the Lord (12:5–11), and who performed many other miracles. And it was Peter in his later years who would comfort the persecuted church with these words of divine wisdom: "Humble yourselves under the mighty hand of God, that He may exalt you in due time, casting all your care upon Him, for He cares for you" (1 Peter 5:6–7).

GOD HAS A PLAN

So why does Jesus ask *us* to step out in faith and walk to Him? Is it so we can tell other people of all our accomplishments? No, He's building our faith to prepare us for greater assignments that await us within the kingdom of God—things that will require an absolute confidence in God to do the impossible. He desires that we grow stronger that we may strengthen the weak. He's in the process of making godly leaders for His people.

Are you one who has looked back with longing eyes to the great stories of the Bible and wished you could have been there? Have you looked back and thought, *I wish I could have been beside Moses at the Red Sea or had a trumpet in my hand at Jericho with Joshua or been part of Gideon's three hundred men. I wish I'd been in the boat that stormy night in Galilee and could have seen Jesus walking on the sea and that I could have walked out to Him side by side with Peter.*

Don't you see Him? Today is *our* day to see the mighty power of God. This is *our* day to walk with the resurrected Jesus. This is the life available to all who would believe.

These are great days to walk with Jesus and see the mighty power of God in our midst. We'll look back upon these days and marvel. But it will take faith; it will take courage.

The apostle Paul understood that the Christian life—the resurrection life—is something fresh and exciting: "Just as Christ was raised from the dead by the glory of the Father, even so we also should walk *in newness of life*" (Romans 6:4). Newness of life! It cannot be the same life you had before you met Christ. It's a completely different existence. It's the place where Jesus walks.

Today is our day to see the mighty power of God.

Only the Lord knows what He wants to do in your life. So ask Him.

Perhaps the Lord is telling you to get out of your comfortable boat. But you're scared. *Trust Him.*

Perhaps you're personally going through a storm. *Keep your eyes on Jesus.*

Perhaps your confidence in God was strong, but now you're distracted and overcome with doubt. *Refocus on Him.*

Impossible situations are normal in the Christian life. This is how God builds our character and brings glory to Himself. The way of resurrection life is an adventurous road. Let's take it!

As you progress in this resurrection life, it not only leads you into an exciting walk with the Lord, it changes you deep inside. It begins to produce in you a Christlike character. You become a living example of the power of the resurrection to bring new life to that which is dead.

CHAPTER 8

RESURRECTION PEACE

Therefore, having been justified by faith, we have
peace with God through our Lord Jesus Christ,
through whom also we have access by faith into this
grace in which we stand, and rejoice in the hope of
the glory of God.

—ROMANS 5:1–2

The first thing we experience in the resurrection life is resurrection peace.

You can always tell those who are walking in a right relationship with Jesus. They're at peace. They're content.

Could anything feel better than to know you're at peace with God?

SAFE IN JESUS' HAND

There's a story of an American Indian who had lived for many years in sin when a Christian missionary led him to Christ. His friends saw such a radical difference that they asked him what happened.

Without saying much, he placed a worm in a pile of leaves, then lit the leaves on fire. The fire grew in size and began to threaten the worm. At the last minute, he plucked the worm out of the fire and said, "Me—that worm."

That's the story of us all. It's not what we've done, but what Christ has done on our behalf. We no longer have to worry about "the fire," but can live by faith that the resurrection has saved us from eternal death.

Anyone who truly understands the meaning of the cross and the resurrection will understand what it means to be at peace with God.

GOOD NEWS/BAD NEWS

In the book of Romans, the apostle Paul captured the essence of the problem of sin and God's provision of salvation. Paul gave a good-news/bad-news scenario.

The bad news: all of us have sinned and fall short of the glory of God. Sin has affected us in such a way that we're no longer right before God, we cannot understand God, we cannot seek God, and we have no fear of God. Left to ourselves, we are doomed to face the punishment of sin.

The good news: Jesus Christ took upon Himself our sin, and

He died in our place. Then the Father raised Him to new life, which we can share. All who believe in Jesus Christ are made right with God, and once that happens, we enjoy a new life.

The result of our faith is peace with God: "Having been justified by faith, we have peace with God through our Lord Jesus Christ" (Romans 5:1).

Peace with God is what people need more than anything else in their lives.

Peace is what people need more than anything else in their lives. But this peace is not like anything we've ever known. It's not primarily an attitude or a peaceful relationship between people, but a state of peace between us and God. We're no longer *His enemies*—we have peace with God, and *we're on His side*!

No Longer Enemies

During World War II, Britain was under the constant threat of new air attacks from the enemy. City lights were blacked out at night. Church bells weren't allowed to ring. But on the day the war with the Nazis finally ended, the lights were turned on, the bells rang cheerfully once again, and people danced in the streets long into the night. Peace brought with it great joy and the freedom to enjoy life once again.

It wouldn't be stretching Paul's words to say that the work of Christ set us free from our state of war existing between God and humans. Paul expressed it this way in his letter to the Colossian church:

> And you, *who once were alienated and enemies* in your mind by wicked works, yet now He has reconciled in the body of His flesh through death, to present you holy, and blameless, and above reproach in His sight. (Colossians 1:21–22)

Before you knew Christ, you were at war with God and in rebellion against the King of kings. But now there is peace. Your soul is no longer struggling; you are right with God. Your status has changed.

You're no longer an enemy of God; you're a child of God.

THE GIFT OF PEACE

The underlying meaning of the biblical word *peace* has to do with relationship. It's "harmony of relationship" or "reconciliation between two parties." It's used four hundred times in the Bible, and it represents the deepest need of the human heart—peace with God.

There's no explaining the sense of peace that comes with a right relationship with God. Jesus said, "Peace I leave with you, My peace I give to you; not as the world gives do I give to you.

Let not your heart be troubled, neither let it be afraid" (John 14:27). His peace is complete; His peace is lasting. His peace comes from knowing that we don't have to cower in the presence of God, but that we can approach Him with confidence.

The gospels tell us of the many times Jesus brought peace to those around Him. He said to a woman who washed His feet, "Your faith has saved you. Go in peace" (Luke 7:50). He said to a woman who was sick for twelve years, "Daughter, be of good cheer; your faith has made you well. Go in peace" (8:48). He said to a raging storm on the Sea of Galilee, "Peace, be still!" (Mark 4:39). He said to the frightened disciples in the upper room, "Peace I leave with you" (John 14:27). And He says to you and me, "Peace I leave with you."

We all want peace, but few are willing to do what's necessary to obtain it.

He wants you to be at peace, so why do so many lack peace in their hearts? Why is it that so many are anxious, worried, stressed, restless, and on edge?

It's because we all want peace, but few are willing to do what's necessary to obtain it.

OBEDIENCE AND PEACE

Have you ever had a child who acted as if nothing were wrong when something *was* wrong?

My (Mel's) youngest daughter has occasionally gotten herself into trouble. I remember an occasion at home when I explicitly told her, under the threat of punishment, not to eat any more candy. Fifteen minutes later I noticed that she wasn't around, and her bedroom door was closed. I walked into her room and found her in a pile of empty wrappers with chocolate on her cheeks. Her immediate response was, "Love you, Daddy!" With a big smile she reached up for a hug and said, "You're the best daddy in the whole wide world!"

She knew she was in trouble, but she desperately wanted to be in Dad's good graces. She wanted a harmonious relationship with her dad; she wanted to be at peace with him. Yet she was doing the very thing that hurt the relationship—disobeying him. In fact, the hands reaching up for a hug were covered in chocolate.

As silly as my daughter looked, we do the exact same thing with God. We want peace with Him, yet do the very thing that robs us of peace and hurts our relationship with God. People knowingly disobey God, yet want Him to overlook it and bless their lives. They don't want to worship God on Sunday, yet expect to worship God for eternity in heaven. They literally use God's name as a curse, yet want Him to show kindness toward them on Judgment Day.

Nobody can expect to know the peace *of* God if they're not at peace *with* God.

God has done everything possible for you to know His peace. "For God did not send His Son into the world to condemn the world, but that the world through Him might be saved" (John 3:17).

And the Son whom God gave for our salvation tells us this: "I have come that they may have life…more abundantly" (10:10). Inherent in that statement is the reality that something can hold us back from such abundance, that there's something that can sabotage our potential. The Bible identifies that something as sin. The sin that Jesus came to free you from is actively working against you. It's keeping you from knowing the peace of God.

It's impossible to enjoy the peace of God if you are willfully sinning against Him. That's why the Bible says, "Let us lay aside every weight, and the *sin* which so easily ensnares us, and let us run with endurance the race that is set before us" (Hebrews 12:1).

It's impossible to enjoy God's peace if you're willfully sinning against Him.

It's a struggle that all must overcome: "All have sinned and fall short of the glory of God" (Romans 3:23). But it's a struggle that Christ has already overcome through the resurrection.

HOLINESS AND PEACE

Remember when the Lord sent an angel to the shepherds on the night Jesus was born? The first thing the angel told them was this: "Do not be afraid" (Luke 2:10).

Why were these men afraid? Scripture says that when the angel of the Lord came to the shepherds, "the glory of the Lord shone around them" (verse 9). What is the glory of the Lord?

In the Old Testament, when the glory of the Lord shone, it laid bare moral secrets and revealed the innermost parts of people.

Isaiah was a good man who was preparing to serve the Lord. But when the Lord's glory shone around him, he cried out, "Woe is me, for I am undone! Because I am a man of unclean lips, and I dwell in the midst of a people of unclean lips" (Isaiah 6:5).

Daniel was the most righteous man of his day, but when the glory of the Lord came to him in a "great vision," his response was this: "No strength remained in me; for my vigor was turned to frailty in me, and I retained no strength.... Suddenly, a hand touched me, which made me tremble on my knees" (Daniel 10:8, 10).

These men were afraid. Though they couldn't tell exactly what was going on, they knew they were in the presence of God's glory. His glory shone bright, revealing the darkest corners, unveiling the darkest territories of their own souls. They were filled with fear, for they knew a sinner could not remain in the presence of a holy God.

When Christ was born and the angel of the Lord appeared to the shepherds and declared, "Do not be afraid," the reason was immediately stated: "For there is born to you this day in the city of David *a Savior,* who is Christ the Lord" (Luke 2:11). The Savior, the Prince of Peace, had come. But if a Savior had *not* been born, then you probably *should* be afraid to see a messenger from God.

If we were to stand before a holy God as people who remain in sin, we ought to be very afraid. God's Word says that the wages of sin is death, so to continue to live in sin is to lose life forever.

So how does God bring peace? He offers forgiveness of sin and a restored relationship. Jesus is the Prince of Peace, but you will know peace only if you make Him Lord of your life.

It's like this. Just because there's abundant bread in a store doesn't mean the hungry man out on the street is satisfied. Just because lakes and rivers are full of water doesn't mean that a man dying in the desert will have his thirst quenched.

Jesus brings peace—if you come to Him on His terms.

In the same way, Jesus brings peace, but to experience it, you must come to Him on His terms. Are you walking in a relationship with Christ that brings peace? It's a choice.

GIVING JESUS CONTROL

I (Mel) spent some time in Texas while in seminary. There was a man in our church who trained cutting horses for a living. I wasn't an accomplished rider by any stretch of the imagination, but he gave me the opportunity to ride one of his horses.

When I mounted the horse, it was unlike anything I'd experienced before. I immediately lost control, and the horse started spinning in circles, moving around with lightning speed. Everything I did to correct things just seemed to make it worse.

I finally realized that the struggles I was having were not the horse's problem, but mine. This horse was worth sixty thousand dollars and was so well trained that it responded to every move I made. It was my own actions that were causing him to jump around. My attempt to ride smoothly was actually what made the ride very dangerous.

Many people who struggle in life—whose ride is pretty bumpy and dangerous—don't realize that they're experiencing the results of their own actions. Sin breaks the relationship and robs you of peace.

We need to give the reins of our lives over to God…and He will bring peace.

PEACE BRINGS ACCESS

After Paul described the peace we have with God through Jesus Christ, he went on to say that through Jesus we also "have access by faith into this grace in which we stand, and rejoice in the hope of the glory of God" (Romans 5:2). It's one thing to know you're at peace with God; it's another to know that you have *access* to Him.

The word *access* signifies "the act of bringing or introducing."

Peace with God—through a relationship with Christ—will introduce us to the grace of God. The peace of Christ brings us into the sphere of God's grace in which we stand before Him.

You may not understand what a radical change this represented from the way the Jews had always experienced their relationship with God. Of all the people of Israel, only the high priest could enter the holy of holies, the presence of God. Once a year, on the Day of Atonement, the priest acted as the people's representative. While everyone else waited outside, the priest went inside the holy of holies. He would sprinkle blood upon the mercy seat to atone for the people's sin. Even after the sacrifices had been made, those who had been forgiven of their sin still could not enter the holy of holies. Instead, they all went home. The priest would walk out and close the curtain, and it would be another year before anyone entered again.

What a difference Christ has made! We don't stand outside while a priest goes to God on our behalf. Rather, we stand *within* the holy of holies, ushered into the presence of God's grace through Jesus Christ:

> Having boldness to enter the Holiest by the blood of
> Jesus, by a new and living way which He consecrated for
> us, through the veil, that is, His flesh, and having a High
> Priest over the house of God, let us draw near with a true
> heart in full assurance of faith, having our hearts sprinkled

from an evil conscience and our bodies washed with pure water. (Hebrews 10:19–22)

The peace Christ accomplished on our behalf brings us literally into a personal relationship with the holy God. Our Savior's death and resurrection tore down the barrier of sin and ushers us into the holy of holies.

ONLY ONE WAY TO PEACE WITH GOD

We all want peace in our lives. But understand this: Jesus Christ is the *only* access to God and therefore the only source of lasting peace. Don't believe anyone who tells you there are many ways to God. Don't believe anyone who says, "As long as you're sincere in your belief…"

Don't believe anyone who tells you there are many ways to God.

Men seem to have an aversion to reading maps. After all, we have confidence in our innate sense of direction—we don't need others telling us the way. If you're a man, you've probably been on a trip where you were absolutely certain you knew the way—there was no doubt in your mind. Though everything within you said to turn right, your wife was telling you to turn left. What did you do? Of course you turned right, for being wrong wasn't an option for you. Your wife got silent and waited to see how long you'd go before discovering your mistake and turning around. Yes, you were *sincere* in your convictions. But unfortunately, you were sincerely wrong.

It doesn't matter what you "sincerely" believe. All that matters is whether what you believe is actually true. And when it comes to salvation, Jesus is the only truth. He said, "I am the way, the truth, and the life. No one comes to the Father except through Me" (John 14:6).

Is there a need for repentance in your life because of your "sincere" mistakes? That word *repentance* means we must turn around and go with Jesus. He gives us peace with God as well as access into God's presence.

Do *you* have peace? Have you been introduced to almighty God? Do you have hope in this life and the life hereafter?

You can. It comes when you put your faith in Jesus Christ as Lord and Savior. It's not a one-time commitment to Christ; it's a daily walking with Christ as Lord. You cannot come to God on your own; you come *with Christ*. He is the Prince of Peace.

CHAPTER 9

RESURRECTION JOY

So they went out quickly from the tomb with fear
and great joy, and ran to bring His disciples word.
—MATTHEW 28:8

I n Matthew's description of the resurrection event, he told how the women "went out quickly from the tomb with fear and great joy" (Matthew 28:8). This "fear and great joy" is contrasted with the Roman soldiers, who "shook for fear of him, and became like dead men" (verse 4).

The word *fear* was used in both cases, but it wasn't the same fear. For the soldiers, their fear paralyzed them. But for the women, their fear energized them—something was in the air, and deep inside, their spirits leaped with inexpressible joy. Jesus was alive!

For those in rebellion against God, fear brings terror at the sight of a divine messenger of God. To those in right relationship to God, fear redirects our attention from self to the awe-inspiring God we love, and we can share in the "great joy" over the never-ending good news of the resurrected Christ.

The last words in the gospel of Luke display this same emotion. After the disciples watched their risen Lord ascend back into heaven, "they worshiped Him, and returned to Jerusalem *with great joy*, and were continually in the temple praising and blessing God" (Luke 24:52–53). The disciples were filled with not just joy, but "great joy." This was beyond their wildest imagination; this was something that absolutely turned their lives upside down.

JOY OF THE LORD

The Lord wants the resurrection to produce great joy in our lives. John's gospel makes this abundantly clear.

Consider the high priestly prayer of Jesus in John 17, where He poured out His heart to the heavenly Father. This was a very tender moment in the final hours before Jesus would endure the betrayal of a friend, illegal trials at the hands of "religious leaders," unmerciful beatings, and the excruciating pain of the crucifixion. "The hour has come," He said (verse 1). Yet even now He was thinking of His disciples. He thought of those He would leave behind once His time on earth was over.

After talking with the Father about His assignment to carry the sin of the world on the cross, Jesus turned His prayers toward these disciples. The first thing He prayed for them was this: "I come to You, and these things I speak in the world, that they may have *My joy* fulfilled in themselves" (verse 13).

Think of this moment: He is about to endure the pain of the cross, and He wants His disciples to be full of *joy*!

As He was about to endure the pain of the cross, He wanted His disciples to be full of joy!

When you consider those early disciples who would carry on the work of the Lord after He left, this prayer is quite amazing. Notice that Jesus did not pray, "Father, make them to be great preachers, for they will proclaim the gospel." He did not pray, "Father, give them insight to teach theology to those who will come." No, their joy was on the heart of Jesus. "Father, place *My joy* in them, that *their joy* may be made full."

Why was the Lord so concerned that they be full of joy? Because He knew that the message they would preach would mean nothing if they weren't full of joy. If the resurrection did not make a qualitative difference in their lives, why would anyone want to hear the gospel? But He knew that a joyful life and the corresponding countenance on their faces would convince people of the reality of freedom from sin and hope in Christ.

JOY OF THE LORD IS STRENGTH

Jesus also knew that there would be many difficult days ahead for the disciples, and the world would watch to see how they would respond to those difficulties.

The disciples would prove that a relationship with God brings joy, and everything else pales in comparison to a relationship with the risen Christ. "Cast insults at me, and revile me, but God is near. Throw me in prison, but God is near. Stone me and beat me, but the nearness of God is my good." They would not exchange salvation for anything on earth. A relationship with Christ brings joy, and nothing on earth can take that away.

People would hear the gospel and believe it because of the *look in the eyes* of those who proclaimed it.

That's why Jesus was concerned about joy in the disciples' lives. And that joy was exactly what the resurrection produced in their lives. Listen to some of the descriptions in Acts of their lives after Christ rose from the dead:

> So they departed from the presence of the council, *rejoicing* that they were counted worthy to suffer shame for His name. (5:41)

> And the disciples were filled with *joy* and with the Holy Spirit. (13:52)

Paul said,

But none of these things move me; nor do I count my life dear to myself, so that I may finish my race with *joy*, and the ministry which I received from the Lord Jesus, to testify to the gospel of the grace of God. (20:24)

Listen as well to what the apostles taught the early church, out of their own experience of resurrection joy:

Rejoice in the Lord always. Again I will say, *rejoice*! (Philippians 4:4)

Count it all *joy* when you fall into various trials. (James 1:2)

Though now you do not see Him, yet believing, you *rejoice* with *joy inexpressible* and full of glory. (1 Peter 1:8)

But *rejoice* to the extent that you partake of Christ's sufferings, that when His glory is revealed, you may also *be glad* with *exceeding joy*. (1 Peter 4:13)

These things we write to you that your *joy* may be full. (1 John 1:4)

Let us suggest that if you've lost the joy of the Lord, you've lost sight of the resurrected Lord. I'm not talking about losing your salvation, but losing the *joy* of your salvation. If you've lost the joy of serving the Lord, you're in trouble! It's an indication that you've moved away from Him, that you're no longer filled with His Spirit.

If you've lost the joy of the Lord, you've lost sight of the resurrected Lord.

The sense of joy that comes from an encounter with the risen Lord grows only deeper as you walk with Him. Once you come to know peace with God, joy springs forth like an ever-flowing well.

The Christian life is not just an emotion. But how can you receive forgiveness for every sin you've ever committed, experience absolute peace with a holy God, have assurance of salvation and a home in heaven, know victory over temptations to sin, and walk in fellowship with Jesus Christ—yet not have joy?

The resurrection life is one characterized by joy. It can be no other way.

BEYOND EMOTION

Happiness is fleeting; it's completely regulated by your present circumstances. Not so with the joy of the Lord. His joy resides deep inside your life and is determined by relationship, not circumstantial realities.

Abiding joy is clear evidence that you have peace with God and are experiencing a deep relationship with the living Christ. A person walking with the Lord is a realist. He or she understands the seriousness of life and the reality of spiritual warfare, but that doesn't rob that person of joy. No, as long as the Lord is present in a believer's life, they'll have His joy.

If you've figured this out, then being a Christian is not the drudgery of following God's law. It isn't all hellfire and brimstone and the absence of all fun. Yes, the Christian life requires dealing with eternally serious issues in life, but Christ is the answer to those issues, and that's what brings such joy; it's what produces abundant life in Christ. When Christ forgives your sin and fills you with His Spirit, you ought to know the joy of the Lord.

Paul's prayer for the Colossians was that they would experience "all patience and longsuffering *with joy;* giving thanks to the Father who has qualified us to be partakers of the inheritance of the saints in the light" (1:11–12). Then Paul stated the reason for this joy and thanksgiving: "He has delivered us from the power of darkness and conveyed us into the kingdom of the Son of His love, in whom we have redemption through His blood, the forgiveness of sins" (verses 13–14).

That's the experience of every believer. They're taken out of darkness and into the presence of the Lord, who brings light into their lives. This is the basis for a joy that comes not from circumstances, but from inside where the risen Lord reigns.

I (Mel) once had a deacon come to me with a concern over a situation in the church that we needed to deal with. He was

People live in sin yet want God's blessing.

concerned that a couple was missing out on the abundant life that God desired for them to know. It was a scene that seems to happen over and over again in churches today—people living in sin, yet wanting God's blessing.

When we went to the couple's home and challenged them to adjust their lives to God's standard, they responded with complete obedience. The result was God's immediate blessing. Not only did He miraculously work out some difficult circumstances in their lives, but there was a significant change inside them. The woman described how she'd been riddled with guilt and shame, that she struggled with anxiety and depression. But after she repented, she said with joy in her eyes, "I slept like a baby all night for the first time in six months." She now had peace with God and was filled with joy. She experienced what Peter spoke of: "Repent therefore and be converted, that your sins may be blotted out, so that *times of refreshing* may come from the presence of the Lord" (Acts 3:19). Her relationship with the living Lord was restored, and she experienced the refreshing joy of His presence.

Some have the idea that *repentance* is a harsh word. They envision an old, white-haired preacher thundering away and pounding on a pulpit, scaring people into walking down to the altar, where they must turn or burn! Quite the contrary, *repent-ance* is the most positive word in the Bible. It simply means to turn *away from* that which will destroy your life and *toward* that which will bring abundant life. It's turning *from* sin and death and *toward* Christ and forgiveness. Once a person repents of their sin and chooses to make Christ the Lord of their life, they immediately experience times of refreshing in their soul.

True Joy

There are many kinds of things that bring joy into our lives. But nothing compares with the joy of the Lord. Humor and laughter are both wonderful and necessary parts of experiencing life to its fullest. A great story can change the atmosphere of a room, filling it with laughter. *But this is not the joy of the Lord.* We can know the joy of entering a beautiful church building and singing wonderful songs of worship, getting caught up in an emotional lift through stirring and powerful music. *But this is not the joy of the Lord.* There's joy that comes simply from being with believers you've come to love and cherish. *But this is not the joy of the Lord.* There's joy from reading comforting words from Scripture, hearing truth from God's Word that touches the soul. *But this is not the joy of the Lord.*

None of these things are *opposed* to resurrection joy. They are, however, poor substitutes for what we're talking about. There's a danger of thinking they're the same thing, that they're all there is to the Christian life. For we may enjoy life while at the same time living void of the joy of the Lord.

We may enjoy life while at the same time living void of the joy of the Lord.

The deepest expression of resurrection joy can come only from the resurrected Christ. It's a by-product of the love relationship you have with Him. Can humor and frivolity compare to the joy that comes from the One who gives abundant life? Can a song about the Lord compare to actually talking with Him? Can time in the Scriptures compare to time spent with the One to whom the Scriptures point us?

For sure, a genuine relationship with Christ *will* produce Christian fellowship, heartfelt singing, the study of His Word, and intimate times of prayer. But never let these activities be a substitute for the relationship. Jesus is not a doctrine to believe in; He has been resurrected, and He offers a real and personal relationship to all who come to Him.

ABIDING JOY

Jesus told us how to find the resurrection joy. He knew He would always be our source of joy.

One of the most intimate teachings He gave to the disciples

was about the abiding relationship of the vine and the branches. Listen carefully to this disclosure of our source of joy:

> I am the vine, you are the branches. He who abides in Me, and I in him, bears much fruit; for without Me you can do nothing.... As the Father loved Me, I also have loved you; abide in My love. If you keep My commandments, you will abide in My love, just as I have kept My Father's commandments and abide in His love. These things I have spoken to you, that My joy may remain in you, and that your joy may be full. (John 15:5, 9–11)

This is the abiding relationship with Christ that brings His joy into our lives. Joy flows through Him into us.

There's not a way in the world you can know the joy of the Lord without abiding in Him. That requires time with Him; it necessitates a diligent prayer life. You cannot abide in Him without talking with Him and listening to Him.

He doesn't just give you joy; He *is* your joy. If you ever become "detached" from the vine, you'll automatically wither and lose your joy. You cannot produce such joy on your own any more than a branch that has been cut off can produce fruit on its own. Instead, quite the opposite happens. You become brittle, dry, and hard. You lose the life that produces fruit.

Joy is the fruit of the abiding relationship with Christ.

CONFIDENT JOY

Do you know why we can have joy in all circumstances of life? Why we can be optimistic and positive in life?

It's because we're walking with the resurrected Lord. We know He is sovereign and on His throne. He's in absolute control of all things. Furthermore, we know that He sees what we don't see. He has the big picture and knows what's coming. And we already know that He loves us. And to know that the Father has given Jesus all authority in heaven and on earth means that we're in good hands.

Paul said, "We know that all things work together for good to those who love God, to those who are the called according to His purpose" (Romans 8:28). This verse doesn't say, "All things work out just like we want them to." But it reminds us that God is in control. God is fulfilling His purposes in our lives. We can have joy because we trust that God's will for our lives is best.

LIGHTEN UP

There are times when the Lord is probably telling us, "Lighten up! Don't be so uptight all the time! Why so downcast? Why so sad? Why do you act like serving Me is so terrible?"

We have the privilege of sharing the good news! How can we do it with a downcast spirit? For a downcast spirit says, "I don't trust God with this situation." It's like admitting, "There is no good news."

The world needs to see the good news in action. They need to see abundant life in Christ!

If joy is present deep down in your heart, it cannot be hidden. It will even-

A downcast spirit says, "I don't trust God with this situation." It's like admitting, "There is no good news."

tually show up on your face. If you haven't seen it in a while, perhaps you need to make sure it's even there. It ought to be expressed in the words you say, the tone of your voice, and the look in your eyes. It ought to be known in the way you sing. Joy will find its way into your relationships, both with intimate friends and with strangers. People ought to look forward to your greeting, for they know that you'll encourage their lives with a joyful encounter.

Indeed, the joy of the Lord as experienced by the apostles was a validation of the message of the gospel. We hear them say, "To live is Christ, and to die is gain" (Philippians 1:21). And we see them singing while in the depths of a horrific prison (Acts 16:23–25).

Paul challenges us, "Only let your conduct be worthy of the gospel of Christ" (Philippians 1:27). Are you living worthy of the gospel? Does your life demonstrate the *good news* of God? If you truly know the joy of the Lord, your countenance will testify that you've met the risen Lord.

Paul understood joy as a state of mind characterized by peace. It was a confidence in life that was rooted in faith. It resulted from a keen awareness that the risen Lord was present. Paul's understanding of joy was more than an emotion or feeling; it was the ability to see beyond any particular event to the sovereign Lord who stands above all events and ultimately has control over them.

When you realize that joy is the fruit of a relationship, not of an activity, then you have the ability to rejoice in the Lord always. For you're experiencing the perfect fulfillment of that for which God created you.

So "rejoice in the Lord always. Again I will say, rejoice!" (Philippians 4:4).

CHAPTER 10

RESURRECTION POWER

And with great power the apostles gave witness to the resurrection of the Lord Jesus. And great grace was upon them all.

—ACTS 4:33

Power. It's something all nations of the world seek. It's something people have fought over since the beginning of time. Meanwhile, nations rise and fall; people come and go.

And then there is God—the One who has power over all things. "How awesome are Your works!" the psalmist declared to Him. "Through the greatness of Your power Your enemies shall submit themselves to You" (Psalm 66:3). There's no one who can stand against almighty God, no principality or power that can even be compared to His supremacy. "God has spoken once, twice I have heard this: that *power belongs to God*" (62:11).

POWER OF LIFE

Paul mentioned power very early in his letter to the Romans. "I am not ashamed of the gospel of Christ, for it is *the power of God* to salvation for everyone who believes" (1:16). The word *power* in this verse is a translation of the Greek word *dúnamis.* You can easily recognize there the roots of the English word *dynamite.*

Many preachers have stirred up their listeners by declaring that the gospel is God's *dynamite* for salvation. Its explosive power can transform a life in dramatic fashion. But using such an illustration forces our picture of dynamite back into Paul's words—something he had no intention of saying. Paul neither had a concept of dynamite as we now know it, nor would he use it as an illustration of resurrection power. Dynamite demolishes, breaks apart, and can even take life. But the gospel of Christ does exactly the opposite of dynamite. Paul is expressing how the power of the gospel brings wholeness and gives new life.

The greatest power on earth is to give life to the dead, and God alone holds such power.

Which has more power—that which takes life or that which gives life? The greatest power on earth is to give life to that which is dead, and God alone holds such power.

The resurrection is the best and clearest demonstration of an astounding power that comes from God's presence. This is the power that gave new life to Jesus once He had publicly been crucified and had physical life taken from Him. *Life* is the essential nature of resurrection power.

The same is true today. Resurrection power always has to do with *life*. And God has placed this exact same power within every believer. He intends to bring life through those who have come to experience abundant life in Christ.

BELIEVE IT—RECEIVE IT

Among Jesus' last words to the disciples was this promise: "You shall receive *power* when the Holy Spirit has come upon you" (Acts 1:8). That promise was fulfilled, and the early church came to know the power that brings life.

Listen to more New Testament teaching about the power given to all who put their faith in the resurrected Christ:

> For the message of the cross is foolishness to those who are perishing, but to us who are being saved it is the *power of God.* (1 Corinthians 1:18)

> And my speech and my preaching were not with persuasive words of human wisdom, but in demonstration of the Spirit and of *power,* that your faith should not be in the wisdom of men but in *the power of God.* (1 Corinthians 2:4–5)

For the kingdom of God is not in word but in *power*.
(1 Corinthians 4:20)

But we have this treasure in earthen vessels, that the excellence of the *power* may be of God and not of us.
(2 Corinthians 4:7)

Now to Him who is able to do exceedingly abundantly above all that we ask or think, according to the *power* that works in us.... (Ephesians 3:20)

...that I may know Him and the *power* of His resurrection, and the fellowship of His sufferings. (Philippians 3:10)

Over and over we're told of a power given to believers in Jesus. But do we experience it? Are we living in that power? Or have we become satisfied with giving God our best, missing out on a power given to us the moment we believed in the resurrected Lord?

Perhaps we need to understand more about this power from the Lord's perspective. This power is for "everyone who believes." It's at work in those "who are being saved." It's the basis of our faith and the living expression of our words. It's contained in earthen vessels, it's at work within us, and it's the desire of our lives.

Listen carefully to what Paul says about power in his prayer for the believers in Ephesus. He prayed for their eyes to be enlightened for this purpose:

> …that you may know…the exceeding greatness of His
> power toward us who believe, according to the working of
> His *mighty power* which He worked in Christ when He
> raised Him from the dead and seated Him at His right
> hand in the heavenly places, far above all principality and
> *power* and might and dominion, and every name that is
> named, not only in this age but also in that which is to
> come. And He put all things under His feet, and gave Him
> to be head over all things to the church, which is His body,
> the fullness of Him who fills all in all. (Ephesians 1:18–23)

It seems that the Ephesian Christians did not fully understand who they were or what they'd received at salvation. So Paul prayed for their understanding to grasp the magnitude of what Christ accomplished on their behalf.

The power that raised Jesus from the dead and gave Him authority over all things is the same power *we* should experience as believers. This power that defeated sin was to be experienced not in heaven but on earth. This power that broke the rule of Satan was for the

The power that raised Jesus from the dead is the same power we should experience as believers.

purpose of freeing people in this world from his authority. This power is to be realized in us and through *us*.

His power, *His* strength, *His* might, *His* authority is to permeate the church. For Christ has been made head of the church, and we are His body. The church is both the object of His blessing and the instrument through which He touches the world.

ESSENTIAL POWER

Resurrection power is very practical in expression but spiritual in nature. Just as life and death must be seen from eternity's perspective, we must understand divine power the same way. Sure, God can do spectacular miracles and control the physical universe with just a word, but that's not His priority. His greatest power is displayed not in the natural realm, but in that which is supernatural and impacts eternity. While God may choose to bring back physical health and restore a diseased or injured human body, the greatest miracle of God is what He does to the soul that is dead. He has the power to give eternal life—He revives the spirit within us by breathing new life into us, lifting us to a place much higher than ever imagined. He brings us to Himself, and we live in the presence of the holy. And in that place, we experience the divine (2 Peter 1:4).

During the Welsh Revival of 1904, a newspaper reporter was sent to do a story on this movement that was causing such a stir.

Upon arriving at the train station in Cardiff, he excitedly asked a railway attendant, "Where is the Revival, please? Where can I find it?"

"In here, sir." The man smiled as he pointed to his heart.

Where does a great movement of God take place? Where does revival happen? Where does new life come? Not in buildings, not in cities, not in any place...but only in the hearts of people.

When we pray for a great move of God's power, don't look around for it; look within. God's greatest miracles are found in the human soul.

God's greatest miracles are found in the human soul.

The power of the resurrection is not necessarily seen in large church buildings, crowds of people, or a multitude of ministries for the community. All those things are fine but have nothing to do with the power of the resurrection. In fact, all those things may be present in a church, yet that church may completely miss out on God's purposes.

God is not impressed by large churches or small churches. The size of a church doesn't determine the moral and spiritual condition of a community. There are churches of various types all over the land, yet crime persists, abortion continues at an alarming rate, divorce still destroys families, pornography is on the rise, anxiety and stress immobilize many, and suicide takes more lives.

But Paul said, "The kingdom of God is not in word but in

power" (1 Corinthians 4:20). All across the land there are many words—but little power.

We'll know we're in the center of God's will and living according to His purpose when we see His power working in us and through us to bring transformation to people and entire communities. God is not impressed by any of *our* accomplishments, for *our* activity is limited in effect. There are things we cannot do and needs we cannot meet. In fact, we cannot save anybody. We cannot give anyone eternal life and a home in heaven. When it comes to the most important things in life, we fall short. Only Christ can set people free. And when He sets them free, they are free indeed (John 8:36).

POWER FOR LIVING

We can talk about Christ all we want, but that doesn't mean we know His presence. The testimony of the early church is that a pure and simple faith in Christ is what really matters. The glory of the early church was that men and women proclaimed the gospel with power—and certified it by holy lives.

Listen to this description of the early church:

> And when they had prayed, the place where they were
> assembled together was shaken; and they were all filled
> with the Holy Spirit, and they spoke the word of God

with boldness.... And with *great power* the apostles gave witness to the resurrection of the Lord Jesus. And great grace was upon them all. (Acts 4:31, 33)

What strikes us most about the power of the early church is not so much its success, but the fact that success happened with limited resources for a task of such eternal consequence. The early church consisted of plain men and women who were both insignificant and unknown. It began with no equipment or resources like we enjoy today. It fought against fierce persecution and hatred, yet had the power to turn the world upside down (Acts 17:6). Persecution fell upon these early Christians with a fury, yet they emerged stronger and more powerful than any movement the world had known.

Such power was the realized impact of the resurrection. Victory was already won, and the early believers claimed it as their own in the name of Jesus.

POWER THAT MATTERS

From eternity's perspective, don't get distracted from the real power available. Satan will distract you at this point, for our human nature wants to see a lot of visible, ecstatic miracles that impact the world around us. As a result, we don't celebrate the greatest power on earth—to see a person become born again.

Why do we marvel over a man healed of cancer, yet almost ignore a young boy who gives his life to Christ? That man will eventually die of some disease or another, but the boy will live forever.

Consider Jesus' encounter with the lame man whose friends brought him to Jesus for healing (Luke 5:17–26). It was a dramatic scene that lets us see the reason Jesus came to this earth and to observe the power in His life.

On that day when the paralytic was brought by his friends to be healed, they couldn't make their way to Jesus because the crowd listening to Him teach was so dense. The friends were so desperate to find healing for the man that they climbed on the housetop, pulled back the roof to gain access, then lowered the man down from above.

Can you picture the scene from inside? Dust starts falling from the ceiling, then chunks of rubble drop, then daylight bursts into the room, and down floats a man. The look on the man's face must have reflected his desperate hope. The faces of his friends peering in from the hole above must have looked expectant. And the face of Jesus must have been full of compassion. Can you see His smile as He realized the faith of these men?

Jesus responded to their faith with a shocking statement: "Man, your sins are forgiven you." Where did that come from? The man wanted to walk, yet Jesus didn't even address his physical condition. Instead, He forgave the man's sins.

Hearing this, the Pharisees present in the crowd were enraged. "Who is this who speaks blasphemies? Who can forgive sins but God alone?"

Jesus had done for the man more than he had asked. Jesus demonstrated His power to release the man from sin and cleanse his life. But what happens deep in someone's soul is not always immediately seen, at least through human eyes. So He made another profound statement:

> "Which is easier, to say, 'Your sins are forgiven you,' or to say, 'Rise up and walk'? But that you may know that the Son of Man has power on earth to forgive sins"—He said to the man who was paralyzed, "I say to you, arise, take up your bed, and go to your house." Immediately he rose up before them, took up what he had been lying on, and departed to his own house, glorifying God. (verses 23–25)

According to Jesus, it takes far more power to forgive sins than it does to heal the physically infirm. From an earthly perspective, He had the power to heal the man of paralysis and give him a higher quality of life. From an eternal perspective, He did a far greater miracle. He forgave the man's sin and cleansed his soul.

Forgiving sin required an all-encompassing and life-giving expression of power.

Physical healing required not power but a casual word. Forgiving sin, however, required an all-encompassing and life-giving expression of power. The cross and resurrection represent such a powerful moment in time that both the physical and spiritual world shook.

What if Jesus, when He came to earth, had healed the lame, the lepers, and the blind, yet never conquered sin in the cross and resurrection? Those He ministered to would have experienced longer and healthier lives, but they would still have died and gone into eternity with no hope. We too would have had no benefit from His time on earth.

Fortunately, Jesus was not distracted from the priority of eternity. Resurrection power primarily has to do with eternal life. This is true for Jesus, and it should be true for us.

DON'T GET DISTRACTED

Satan doesn't mind if we witness the physical miracles that give us a more enjoyable life on earth—as long as we still die in our sins. He has made many people comfortable on earth who will be uncomfortable for all eternity.

Hear this carefully. As a believer in Jesus Christ, you have the power to give the gift of eternal life. Not because of who you are, but because the resurrected Jesus dwells within every Christian. *He* has conquered sin and death and is ready to share His victory through your life. But Satan will do everything possible to keep you from that truth. He wants to keep your focus on the physical world and leave the spiritual world a mystery that's left for a future experience in heaven. He wants us to keep truth locked in our heads—and distant from everyday reality.

You can always tell when someone hasn't experienced the resurrection. They're still working hard in their own power to serve God. They haven't learned to let the risen Christ live through their life. Instead, they do their best to help people. It isn't that they don't care, or even that they don't love others. The problem is that they still think the resurrection is something they'll experience only when they die and need a new body for their days in heaven. So they work hard in their own strength because they believe that's all the strength they possess. Oh, they may believe "theologically" that they're a "new creation" in Christ, but they have no idea what this means in daily life. As a result, the world gets the best *we* have to offer and misses out on the best *God* has to offer.

Ministries that meet felt needs among people are good; Jesus healed many people while He walked the earth. Such ministries often touch our natural emotions and open the door for a spiritual touch. True love cannot look the other way when there's the capacity to help someone in a destitute or unhealthy condition. But God's love cannot stay there—it must go further. It must meet people's ultimate need, whether they're aware of their spiritual need or not.

Jesus said that those who remain in their sin will surely die (John 8:24). So He died in our place and went to the grave—but

The power of almighty God ripped His Son from the eternal chains meant for you and me.

with the full confidence that the power of the Father was sufficient. And indeed, the Father went after Him and reached down into the darkness and laid hold of His Son. With all the power of Satan and his demons straining to secure the grave, the righteous right hand of the Father found its way. And the power of almighty God ripped His Son from the eternal chains meant for you and me. The resurrection power pulled Him from a pit of darkness back into the kingdom of light.

Praise be to God! Jesus now reigns over the kingdom of light and has complete dominion over all principalities and powers. Talk about power! It all belongs to Jesus. And the same power that raised Jesus from the dead is now in His hands. Anytime a person cries out to Jesus in repentance and pleads for forgiveness of sin, He hears. He has been there; He knows the way to rescue your soul.

And He's coming for those who love Him, for those who believe in the power of His name. Listen to these words of Paul, and rejoice in the power of the resurrection:

He has delivered us from the power of darkness and conveyed us into the kingdom of the Son of His love, in whom we have redemption through His blood, the forgiveness of sins. He is the image of the invisible God, the firstborn over all creation. For by Him all things were created that are in heaven and that are on earth, visible and invisible, whether thrones or dominions or principalities or powers. All things were created through Him and for Him. And He is before all things, and in Him all things consist. And He is the head of the body, the church, who is the beginning, the firstborn from the dead, that in all things He may have the preeminence. (Colossians 1:13–18)

Never lose the wonder of resurrection power! Never look at a new believer with a casual attitude that diminishes the power of the gospel. Rejoice in the miracle of new birth, and remember the cost of salvation.

Herein is the power of the resurrection: "You He made alive, who were dead in trespasses and sins" (Ephesians 2:1).

CHAPTER 11

RESURRECTION AUTHORITY

> *Jesus came and spoke to them, saying, "All authority*
> *has been given to Me in heaven and on earth. Go*
> *therefore and make disciples of all the nations, bap-*
> *tizing them in the name of the Father and of the Son*
> *and of the Holy Spirit, teaching them to observe all*
> *things that I have commanded you; and lo, I am*
> *with you always, even to the end of the age." Amen.*
>
> —MATTHEW 28:18–20

With new life comes new direction. Whereas we used to live according to our own desires and sought to fulfill our own dreams, we do so no longer. Our old life has been cru-cified with Christ, and we're raised to new life in Him.

The mystery of God is this: "Christ in you, the hope of glory" (Colossians 1:27). And now that Christ lives in us, He is our identity. We're in the process of being conformed to His image. We're ambassadors of Christ, and as such, we carry His authority. And with His authority comes His power to give life.

ALL AUTHORITY

As Jesus spoke to His disciples for the last time on earth, He said this: "All authority has been given to Me" (Matthew 28:18). That authority begins with His right to rule your life. His life in you means that you're under His authority. You must respond to the desire of His heart. And His heart is to seek and to save that which is lost. He desires to bring life to that which is dead. And He alone has the authority and the ability to do it.

And what's most amazing about this is that His authority over all things is expressed through the lives of believers:

Then the seventy returned with joy, saying, "Lord, even the demons are subject to us in Your name." And He said to them, "I saw Satan fall like lightning from heaven. Behold, *I give you the authority....*" (Luke 10:17–19)

For in Him dwells all the fullness of the Godhead bodily; and you are complete in Him, who is the head of all principality and power. (Colossians 2:9–10)

And He put all things under His feet, and gave Him to be head over all things to the church, which is His body, the fullness of Him who fills all in all. (Ephesians 1:22–23)

Once we begin to understand that the risen Lord dwells within, we cannot be the same. He has authority over all things, and He is the Lord of our lives. Where He is present, His authority and power are present.

KEYS TO LIFE

Have you ever lost your keys? It's generally followed by losing your mind! It drives you crazy. It usually happens when you're in a hurry and people are waiting on you. So your blood pressure rises and your heart pounds as you frantically tear apart the house looking for those keys.

All the while, your vehicle is sitting in the driveway ready to go. It's gassed up, tuned up, cleaned up, fully equipped to take you anywhere you want to go…but not without keys. Without those, all its potential is useless to you.

I (Mel) recently lost my keys. Actually this wasn't a recent incident; I lost them a long time ago. Fortunately I have another set, but I keep hoping I'll find the first set before I go and buy replacements. The key to my truck has a little computer chip inside, and it's a very expensive key to replace. I could go down and have a key cut to the exact shape of my old key, but it won't work without that component inside. What allows me to use my big diesel 4 x 4 truck isn't just the shape of the key, but the heart of the key.

Let's think more about keys—in particular, the keys to the kingdom of heaven. Jesus said to His disciples, "I will give you the keys of the kingdom of heaven, and whatever you bind on earth will be bound in heaven, and whatever you loose on earth will be

It's what's in our hearts that opens the door into the kingdom of heaven.

loosed in heaven" (Matthew 16:19). You'll soon see that the power of the keys given to us by the Lord does not come from the outward shape of our lives or the form of Christianity we practice. It's what's on the inside; it's what's in our hearts that opens the door into the kingdom of heaven.

Remember, *all* authority has been given to Jesus. And in some way, He has transferred that authority to believers; He has given to us the keys of the kingdom of heaven.

Recall then another passage that refers to the kingdom of heaven. The Lord had earlier taught His disciples to pray, "Our Father in heaven, hallowed be Your name. Your kingdom come. Your will be done on earth as it is in heaven" (Matthew 6:9–10). Then later He told Peter and the disciples, "I will give to you the keys of the kingdom of heaven." By the sovereign will of God, the reign and the rule of God would come to earth through the lives of His disciples. They were given the power to open and close the doors of heaven, the power to loose and to bind what is eternally significant.

In this passage in Matthew 16, Jesus recognized that the Father was working in the life of Peter. The Father had given him keen insight into Jesus' true nature as "the Christ, the Son of the living God" (verse 16). Jesus knew that such divine insight was given to Peter not simply for information or intellectual contemplation. The Father is active in the lives of His people so that they'll adjust their lives to what He's doing in the world around them. What Jesus saw in Peter was not an intelligent and skilled disciple; He saw the Father working.

The Bible says, "The natural man does not receive the things of the Spirit of God, for they are foolishness to him; nor can he know them, because they are spiritually discerned" (1 Corinthians 2:14). The Father had given spiritual discernment to Peter for a purpose, and Jesus conformed to that purpose from the Father by giving Peter and the disciples the keys of the kingdom of heaven.

Jesus was saying, "Peter, it's obvious the Father is working in your life. I, therefore, will entrust to you the keys that will unlock the kingdom of heaven. Your life will be the instrument through which I will bring eternal life to those who are dead in sin." And whether or not Peter fully understood what Jesus was saying, he definitely understood he was being given a profound responsibility. He would be held accountable for what he did with those keys.

ACCOUNTABLE

We discover another side of this eternal responsibility in these words from Jesus on a later occasion:

> Woe to you, scribes and Pharisees, hypocrites! For you shut up the kingdom of heaven against men; for you neither go in yourselves, nor do you allow those who are entering to go in.… Woe to you, scribes and Pharisees, hypocrites! For you are like whitewashed tombs which indeed appear beautiful outwardly, but inside are full of dead men's bones and all uncleanness. (Matthew 23:13, 27)

The religious leaders did not have a genuine relationship with God; they had only the outward appearance. They were all talk and empty words. They were like an attractive burial casket that contained nothing but the horrible consequences of death. There was no life, no spiritual insight. There was no evidence of the activity of the Father. As a result, the Pharisees were keeping people out of the kingdom. They were locking the door. They were like blind men leading thousands of people to follow them over a cliff. They were full of religious words about God, but they didn't know God or have His powerful presence in their lives.

In contrast, Jesus was saying to the disciples, "You will be a part of letting people into the kingdom. You won't just say empty words. Rather, the power of the living God that's at work in your lives will work through you to help others as well."

This would be the strategy of God for all time. Through the lives of transformed people, He would bring salvation to the world. The power of the resurrection that brought life to them would spread through them to those who would encounter their lives.

Do you understand that you've been given the keys of the kingdom? You've been given the "key words" of the gospel that sets people free from sin. The kingdom will come as we receive these keys from the Lord and *use them.*

You've been given the keys of the kingdom—the "key words" of the gospel that sets people free from sin.

As we go into the world under His authority and share the gospel story, the Spirit of God will take those words and convince the world of truth. We're partners with God. We're co-laborers with Him. We've been given the keys to life!

So we must ask ourselves some serious questions. Are we using the keys Christ has given us? Are we going out to share the gospel? Are we living in a manner worthy of the gospel?

If you think about your life and the impact it's making on the world, is there any evidence that you've received the keys of the kingdom of heaven?

Peter not only received the keys, he used them to let many people in. At Pentecost he was filled with resurrection power as he said, "Repent, and let every one of you be baptized in the name of Jesus Christ for the remission of sins; and you shall receive the gift of the Holy Spirit" (Acts 2:38). That day, three thousand souls entered the kingdom of heaven. Peter was using the keys.

Later, Peter and John were at the temple gate and saw a lame man begging for money. Peter told him, "Silver and gold I do not have, but what I do have I give you; In the name of Jesus Christ of Nazareth, rise up and walk" (3:6). He was using the keys.

Peter and the apostles were faithful again to use the keys of the kingdom when they appeared before the Sanhedrin. They'd created quite a stir in Jerusalem, and were brought before the ruling elders to answer for their actions. They were asked, "By what power or by what name have you done this?" (4:7).

Then Peter, filled with the Holy Spirit, said to them, "…by the name of Jesus Christ of Nazareth…. For there is no other name under heaven given among men by which we must be saved." (verses 8, 10, 12)

Peter used the keys! And people were entering into the kingdom left and right.

Where Are the Keys?

How you use the keys of the kingdom will either let people in or keep them out. The power of the resurrection has been entrusted to believers who have met the risen Lord. And the Lord will hold us accountable for how we've used that power.

Jesus said, "Whatever you bind on earth will be bound in heaven, and whatever you loose on earth will be loosed in heaven" (Matthew 16:19). If we leave the keys on the key rack at home, we're closing the doors of heaven to those who are bound by sin.

Jesus said, "He who believes in Him is not condemned; but he who does not believe is condemned already, because he has not believed in the name of the only begotten Son of God" (John 3:18). People are already condemned by their sin; they're already bound by their fallen and sinful nature. Unless somebody sets them free, they'll remain under condemnation.

We can lock the doors to heaven for others in several ways. First, we keep people out by refusing to speak of Jesus. If we refuse to share the gospel, to speak the words of truth that set people free, we're locking heaven's doors and keeping people out. "How then shall they call on Him in whom they have not believed? And how shall they believe in Him of whom they have not heard? And how shall they hear without a preacher?" (Romans 10:14). A preacher is not one who holds a position in a church. A preacher is not a person who is seminary trained and holds the right academic credentials. A preacher is one who has the words of life—one who has received the keys.

Second, we keep people out of heaven by being a stumbling block—when the way we live our lives as Christians becomes a deterrent for people. Anyone who bears the name of Christ must live before a watching world in a Christlike manner. But sometimes others look at the life of a Christian and see the

Anyone who bears the name of Christ must live before a watching world in a Christlike manner.

power of sin, not the power of Christ. Jesus said, "Whoever causes one of these little ones who believe in Me to sin, it would be better for him if a millstone were hung around his neck, and he were drowned in the depth of the sea" (Matthew 18:6).

Third, we keep people out of the kingdom of heaven through disobedience to the Lord. We choose to remain comfortable with our lifestyle and refuse to follow the Lord as He goes to set people free. Perhaps He's asking us to go into mission work, but we won't move to a new place of ministry. As a result, we're not where the Lord wants us to be, and others will not hear through our lives. Or He may want us to teach a Bible study at church or open our home for a small group to meet. But our refusal to step out of our comfort zone means the Lord cannot use us to accomplish His purposes.

There are many ways we can be a hindrance to the work of God, and we'll all be held accountable for how we've responded to His call.

A KEY RELATIONSHIP

So how do you do it? How do you experience the power of the resurrection that unlocks the door to the kingdom of heaven?

It's only through a deep and abiding relationship with the resurrected Christ. Do you have that kind of relationship?

You can experience the power of the resurrection through your relationship with Christ, but you must do three basic things to experience it.

The first step is *repentance*. There's no way to bypass this step. Is there any sin in your life that's hindering your relationship with Christ? Jesus died to forgive your sin, and He rose again to give you victory over it. You cannot remain in sin and experience the power of the resurrection. It's spiritually impossible. You must repent of your sin and ask forgiveness so that your sin may be removed.

Is there any questionable habit or behavior in your life? Get rid of it; run from it; don't let anything weigh you down. Is there any bitterness or ill will toward another? Be reconciled with that person, and seek to live in peace with everyone. Is there still a tendency toward pride and selfish dreams? Put it away, and ask the Lord to give you a humble and contrite spirit.

Even if you find no area of fault, ask the Lord to search your heart and show you any wicked way that may be in your life. If you want resurrection power, you must be cleansed of your sin.

Second, *obey completely* what the Lord is asking of you. Jesus said that the one who loves Him will also obey Him (John 14:21). An intimate love relationship with the Lord is evidenced by obedience to His Word.

Is there anything that you know God wants you to do that you haven't done? Immediately obey. Are there promises you've made to God that you haven't kept? Do what you've promised; make it right. In God's eyes, delayed obedience is disobedience. Do the last thing He told you, and remain in His love.

The third step is to *seek the Lord with all your heart*. Don't be satisfied with past glory, but seek after Him with renewed fervor. Is there a longing to know Him more, or are you content to stay in the comfort zone? How long has it been since you've been refreshed by the presence of God?

Go to Him, run to Him, and search for Him with all your heart. Your relationship with Christ is the key to knowing resurrection power.

CHRIST FIRST

Self is the greatest hindrance in life. Our human nature seeks to rob God of His glory and take it for ourselves. Our natural life is affected by sin—and pride is a thief. Our pride will keep us from ever knowing God's power in our lives, for God will not share His glory with just anyone; He will not use those who can't handle it.

That's why Jesus said that if we want to come after Him—we must deny self (Luke 9:23). Jesus tells us, "I will do the Father's will, I'm carrying out My Father's business to bring the kingdom of God on earth, and I'm going to break the power of sin and release people from Satan's grip. If you want to come after Me, leave your petty complaints and selfish desires behind."

Self says, "Give me great gifts so I can serve You with power." But the Lord shakes His head and says, "You don't understand. I don't give you skills, talents, and power to use as you want. I give you a relationship with Me."

There's a world of difference between our best efforts and the power of the God.

You may have many talents and skills that are being used to serve God. But there's a world of difference between our best efforts and the power of God. That's why Jesus laid the foundation at the very beginning of the call to discipleship: if we want to come after Him and do kingdom work, *we must deny self.*

You are your own worst enemy! The fact that you're trying to please the Lord by working hard is a sign that you're rebelling against the finished work of Christ on the cross and are neglecting the power of the resurrection.

After Peter and the disciples healed a lame man and gave a powerful witness to the rulers of the people, we hear this testimony: "Now when they saw the boldness of Peter and John, and perceived that they were uneducated and untrained men, they marveled. And they realized that they had been with Jesus" (Acts 4:13). The power to transform broken lives comes from one source, and only one source—Jesus Christ.

Do people recognize that we've been with Jesus and He has completely transformed our lives? Do they hear endless words from us about Jesus? Do they sense that we truly know Him?

The world doesn't need to see how good we are, but to see the perfect Son of God in our lives. So is there a recognizable difference in our lives that begs the question, "By what power have you done this?" What is it about your life that makes you different?

We need a personal relationship with Jesus Christ that's real. We need to spend time with Jesus and not be satisfied with a quick little devotional thought for the day.

If you're new in the faith, there's nothing more important than time with the Lord. It will be the best investment of your life. It will bring into your life all that God purposed when He chose to save you. "For all the promises of God in Him are Yes, and in Him Amen, to the glory of God through us" (2 Corinthians 1:20).

And if you've walked with the Lord Jesus for many years, your walk with Him needs to be fresh and alive. You cannot remain in the past; you must actively follow Him. He's not standing still, but is moving forward to do the Father's will. Are you? Are there new things He's teaching you? new opportunities of service He gives you? new people He's blessing through you? Do you have a deep desire to follow Jesus as you did the first day you met Him?

Remember, Jesus doesn't give us power; *He* is our power! It's only in a relationship with Him that you'll see His mighty power working to bring life. And when we walk in a relationship with Him, He gives to us the keys to life.

CHAPTER 12

RESURRECTION CONFIDENCE

What then shall we say to these things? If God is for us, who can be against us?

—ROMANS 8:31

Anyone who has an intimate relationship with Jesus Christ is a person who lives a life of ease. That does not mean life is easy for them but that life is not complicated or stressful. They live with a childlike faith that's absolutely confident in God's love.

"If God is *for* us" (Romans 8:31), then why is there any reason to fear? We don't need to worry about what the future holds, for the hand of God is leading us into the future.

BUILT UPON THE ROCK

Jesus told a parable about house builders. One person built his house upon a rock; the other built it upon sand (Matthew 7:24–27). The same storm came against both houses. That's to be expected, for all houses are out in the elements and contend against nature's way. But when the storm hit, one house stood strong, while the other fell with a great crash. The house on the rock was safe; the house on the sand was destroyed.

Jesus said that storms will come upon all people; some will stand strong, while others will fall. And when the storms come, when the winds blow, when crisis is upon us—the classic question we hear is this: "Why do bad things happen to good people?" Or this: "If God is a God of love, why does He allow tragedy to touch His people?" The theological term for this question is *theodicy*—the attempt to explain how evil can be present in a world that's controlled by a loving God.

Or maybe you've heard it in this simple response: "I thought when I became a Christian, God would take care of me and keep me away from harm and trouble."

When trouble comes, where do you turn?

If you haven't figured it out, trials will find their way into all of our lives. Every last one of us will endure trouble. Sooner or later, it will come. And when it comes, where do you turn? From where do you gain your strength? Have you learned to stand with the risen Lord and enjoy His power to overcome?

Jesus told us, "In the world you will have tribulation; but be of good cheer, I have overcome the world" (John 16:33). There *is* trouble in the world—that's a given. And to endure it, we must go to the One who has overcome it.

BLESSED BY GOD

We could take the time to write here about the question of evil's existence in the world. But there's another question that needs to be addressed first, something that's perhaps more puzzling, more difficult to understand. It's the matter of God's *love* for those who do evil. "God so loved the *world* that he gave His only begotten Son" (John 3:16). How can God love sinners?

In times of suffering, some want to ask, "Why did this terrible thing happen to me?" But we should be asking, "Why does God love me? Why does He forgive me when I sin? Why does He forgive me when I fall into that same sin again? Why does He continue to seek me when I forsake Him? Why does the holy God love a sinful person like me? How could this wonderful thing happen to me?" *Amazing grace, how sweet the sound, that saved a wretch like me. I once was lost, but now am found, was blind but now I see.*

In light of God's love, God's mercy, God's grace—trials and tribulations look much different. As we stand with the risen Lord, the world just seems to take on a new look. So much so that Paul could say, "We also glory in tribulations" (Romans 5:3).

Our greatest problem is that we fail to recognize there's a positive and redemptive purpose to every problem we face. Until we confront this reality, we'll be helpless victims of problems all through our lives.

God is still on His throne! He's still in control! He allows trouble for many different reasons. And the risen Christ is walking with us no matter what comes our way. Our confidence in life is not in our ability to overcome, but in knowing He has overcome.

BLESSED DESPITE THE BAD

So why do trials come?

- *Because we're human and live in a fallen world.* Disasters, troubles, and illness are common on earth.
- *Because we sin or disobey God.* Our bad choices bring undesirable consequences.
- *Because God wants to discipline us.* Parents understand that love means discipline, correction, and training for our children. In the same manner, God uses our trials to instruct and train us in how to walk with Him.

- *Because hard times lead us to the Bible.* They drive us to search God's Word for answers. Trials push us to reestablish priorities and seek truth to guide our lives.
- *Because in moments of crisis, our fellowship with God moves to a deeper level.* Difficulties heighten our dependence upon Him and help us realize that nearness to God is for our good.
- *Because trials teach us to pray with fervency.* Too often we neglect prayer until we encounter suffering.
- And sometimes trials come *because of reasons we don't know.* There are times when God allows trouble, and it doesn't make any sense. But we must choose to trust Him anyway.

We trust God because we're convinced of His love; we trust His heart. And in the midst of suffering, we're drawn closer to the Lord than perhaps at any other time in our lives. This isn't true of everyone, or the whole world would consist of valiant soldiers for the Lord. But to those who trust in God and have learned to walk with Christ, something miraculous happens in their lives through suffering.

When God allows trouble and it doesn't make any sense, we must choose to trust Him anyway.

There's a story of a government official in a country hostile to Christians who once said, "Christians seem to thrive under persecution. Perhaps we should prosper them, and then they would disappear." You see, there's something about persecution that fortifies believers in their faith.

If you came to Christ because you wanted to be free from trouble, you came to the wrong person. Just look at the troubles Paul mentions in his life:

> …in labors more abundant, in stripes above measure, in
> prisons more frequently, in deaths often. From the Jews
> five times I received forty stripes minus one. Three times I
> was beaten with rods; once I was stoned; three times I was
> shipwrecked; a night and a day I have been in the deep; in
> journeys often, in perils of waters, in perils of robbers, in
> perils of my own countrymen, in perils of the Gentiles, in
> perils in the city, in perils in the wilderness, in perils in the
> sea, in perils among false brethren; in weariness and toil,
> in sleeplessness often, in hunger and thirst, in fastings
> often, in cold and nakedness. (2 Corinthians 11:23–27)

Talk about a bad day! Paul endured many storms in life. But in the midst of all his trials, Paul grew stronger in his faith. Christ became his strength. "To this end I also labor, striving according to His working which works in me mightily" (Colossians 1:29).

CONFIDENT IN HIS PRESENCE

As a Christian, you can endure any crisis because of the Lord's hand that protects us.

In the Old Testament, God said,

Fear not, for I am with you;
Be not dismayed, for I am your God.
I will strengthen you,
Yes, I will help you,
I will uphold you with My righteous
    right hand. (Isaiah 41:10)

In the New Testament, Jesus said,

My sheep hear My voice, and I know them, and they follow Me. And I give them eternal life, and they shall never perish; neither shall anyone snatch them out of *My hand.* My Father, who has given them to Me, is greater than all; and no one is able to snatch them out of *My Father's hand.* I and My Father are one. (John 10:27–30)

When the Lord is with you, you can proceed with confidence, knowing that He sees you, that He understands the big picture and that He is aware of all the details in your life. You can rest assured that He has the power to do whatever He desires; miracles are His specialty. He has a purpose for allowing trials into your life, and His actions toward you come from a heart of pure love.

You don't have to fear or let anxiety overcome you; the risen Lord is with you. You never have to say, "Poor me," in His presence. Instead, you'll find yourself saying, "How fortunate I am to have a God who loves me, a God who will never leave me nor forsake me. And how wonderful it will be to someday shed this mortal body and live with Him eternally!"

You never have to say, "Poor me," in His presence.

But you'll never know His peace and live in the confidence of the Lord until you abide in the shadow of the Almighty (Psalm 91:1). The kind of life we're talking about doesn't come to those who run in and out of His presence or who occasionally visit Him. The promises of God are for those who *dwell* in His presence.

Everyone has times of crisis. But some have to anxiously run and find God to help, while others remain in His presence at all times and have His help immediately.

Peace is not just a feeling, but a relationship. Peace will never come from religion, but from relationship with Christ. Peace is not something, but Someone. It's not a feeling or an experience, but the lordship of Christ, the living embodiment of peace.

When Paul says that absolutely nothing "shall be able to separate us from the love of God which is in Christ Jesus our Lord" (Romans 8:39), his words are not just theological rhetoric—they're *true*. You don't have to question God's love; you don't have to question His will. You can trust the heart of God.

We've discovered that it's not just tribulation that upsets our lives; God Himself can turn our world upside down. When God begins to work in mighty power, our lives are unsettled. And only those who are prepared will stand. Only those who are strengthened with His might will be able to endure His activity. God tests our faith through trials to see if we're ready for His mighty work. Just as steel is tested to ensure that it can handle the load of a great bridge, so our faith is tested to see if we can handle the mighty work of God before it comes. When our faith is sure, God pours out His Spirit in power among us.

Just walk with the Lord and you'll be ready for tribulation; you'll be ready for God's Spirit to come in power. And you'll be ready for whatever comes to your life. And by your response, the world will see God. Even more important, *you* will see God living out His purpose in you.

FAMILY TIES

The confidence we know in Christ is found in our new relationship with Him: we're family.

John described it this way: "Behold what manner of love the Father has bestowed on us, that we should be called children

It is because of the resurrection that we become God's children.

of God!" (1 John 3:1). Because of the resurrection, we not only have fellowship with God, we become His children. We're *born of* God. This is not merely external, but a vital *internal* relationship. It's not just having an association with God, but there's a vital union with Him. We're born into the family of God.

It's an awesome privilege to have fellowship with a holy God. How much more to be His child! As the children of God, we stand in a certain position before God. For children, there's a relationship to the parents that entitles them to certain privileges. We stand in a unique and separate relationship to almighty God.

But some people say, "Aren't all people children of God? Didn't God create everybody, and therefore He's the Father of the whole human race?"

The answer: yes...and no!

Yes, God created all people. Yes, we're all derived from the same source and are His handiwork. But *no,* we do not all have the same relationship with God, because we're not all His children.

The Scriptures are clear on this point. Jesus said:

> If God were your Father, you would love Me, for I
> proceeded forth and came from God; nor have I come

of Myself, but He sent Me.… You are of your father
the devil, and the desires of your father you want to
do.… He who is of God hears God's words; therefore
you do not hear, because you are not of God. (John 8:42,
44, 47)

Scripture does not teach that all people are God's children.
There are two relationships we have with God. One is by creation,
the other by salvation. The first is shared by all human beings,
since all belong to God as the Creator. The second is shared only
by those who have been born again—only they belong to God as
their Father. This is accomplished through the death and resurrection of Jesus, and only those who are in a relationship with Him
can be called children of God. Apart from that, we're outside the
family of God and remain dead in trespasses and sins, having none
of the privileges of being His children.

DIVINE NATURE

When John puts an emphasis on being a child of God, he's saying something very significant. A child has a common nature
with the father; a child of God shares the very life of God.

Peter said it this way: "By which have been given to us exceedingly great and precious promises, that through these you
may be partakers of the divine nature" (2 Peter 1:4). To become

partakers of the divine nature is a difficult concept to understand, yet it's everywhere in the New Testament.

In John 15, Jesus talked of the vine and the branches. The branch is "in" the vine, so the life of the vine is passed into the branches—there's an organic relationship.

That's what John is saying when he directs our attention to the love the Father bestows on us: "that we should be called children of God" (1 John 3:1). As children, the life of the heavenly Father is passed into us. We should never think of a Christian as one who is simply trying to live a good life, trying to be better than everyone else, striving to perform certain church rituals, or believing the right doctrines. Christians are children of God; they're born again of the Spirit of God. They've received something of the very nature and life of God Himself. They're transformed people, a new creation. They're absolutely and essentially different from those who have not been born again. John would have us understand that Christians don't merely *act* different; they *are* different.

And how have we been born into the family of God? John answers in an interesting way: "Behold what manner of love *the Father has bestowed on us.*" John moves beyond speaking about love "shown" or "revealed" or "manifested" to us by God to describing how He *bestowed* His love *upon* us. He has put His love *into* us—infused or injected His love within us.

The key word in this verse is *that*—or properly, *in order that.* God bestowed His love upon us for this purpose: that we might become children of God. What really makes us children of God is that He has put His own life into us. God's nature is love,

What really makes us children of God is that He has put His own life into us.

and He put His nature in us so that we possess His love.

That's why the Bible talks so much about Christians loving others. God's love flowing out of us is the evidence that we have God's nature within us—and therefore the proof that we've been born again. As Paul said, "The love of God has been poured out in our hearts by the Holy Spirit who was given to us" (Romans 5:5).

To be a child of God is a great mystery, and the world doesn't understand it. The world ridicules it. It says, "You claim to be God's child! That you've been born again! That you have the Holy Spirit within you! That you share in the divine nature! *You're crazy.*" The world says, "You're not better than us. In fact, you're just an ordinary person like the rest of us." But don't be upset if the world doesn't understand you; it didn't understand Jesus either.

You may not fit into the world around you, but we want you to know something. *You belong.* You're in the family of God. God has no orphans. You belong in His household.

Can there be anything that gives us more confidence in life than to walk with Christ in the family of God?

A LIVING DEMONSTRATION

You can easily tell the people who have been walking with the risen Christ by how they live their lives over time. There's a qualitative difference between the person who has met the risen Lord and the one who has not. Just look at their lives over the long haul. Look how a person grows old.

Those who have known the presence of the Lord will be souls at rest. These people are not anxious or worried about tomorrow; they confidently live day by day in the presence of the Lord. And their lives are making a difference. The power of the resurrection to bring life leaves a trail of transformation wherever they go. By the time their lives on earth are drawing to a close, there's confident expectation of eternity with Christ. Their countenance is full of grace, and the tender spirit of the Lord consumes them. They're a joy to be around; they uplift everyone who knows them. They're living in the joy of their salvation, and they know the presence of Christ.

But those who haven't met the Lord will grow increasingly restless. In their older years, they tend to be known as people whose name starts with *G* and ends with *rumpy,* causing others to keep their distance. They've become frustrated at their inability to make a lasting difference, they become anxious as the end draws near, and they feel helpless to do anything about it.

To be unsure of your relationship with God leaves you unsure about eternity. Fear sets in as you get closer to physical death, for deep inside, your soul knows what lies ahead.

Aren't you glad for the resurrection? You can have confidence that your future is in His hands. He has conquered death and is preparing the rewards of a faithful life.

Confidence—that's what the resurrection brings. Because He lives, so too shall we in the kingdom of heaven.

CHAPTER 13

RESURRECTION HOPE

I do not want you to be ignorant, brethren, concerning those who have fallen asleep, lest you sorrow as others who have no hope. For if we believe that Jesus died and rose again, even so God will bring with Him those who sleep in Jesus.

—1 THESSALONIANS 4:13–14

We've mainly talked of the power of the resurrection in the here and now—its effect upon our life on earth. But oh, there's much more!

For Paul, the present experience of resurrection life is not enough: "If in this life only we have hope in Christ, we are of all men the most pitiable" (1 Corinthians 15:19). Paul's faith was lived out with confidence because he believed that the risen Christ who walked with him in spirit day by day would also someday resurrect for him a new body. The God who raised Jesus from the grave would in like manner raise *us*.

Paul says, "For if we believe that Jesus died and rose again, even so God will bring with Him those who sleep in Jesus" (1 Thessalonians 4:14). One of the most important implications of resurrection is that if we're in relationship with Christ, we no longer have to fear death.

A PLACE CALLED HEAVEN

Can you imagine heaven? Can you even begin to comprehend what life will be like there?

There are many amazing sights to see on this earth God created. You may have looked over the Grand Canyon, descended into Carlsbad Caverns, sat outside late at night and watched the northern lights, or stood on the seashore mesmerized by crashing waves. You may have experienced the joy of marriage or gazed into the eyes of your newborn child as it takes its first breath. The people we've met, the sights we've seen, the wonder of it all—none of it can compare to the hope we have of someday seeing the Lord face to face in a place called heaven.

Can you even begin to comprehend what life in heaven will be like?

Biblical writers tried to express what heaven is like, but how can words describe it? They can't! Words are inadequate. The human language is bankrupt when it comes to describing heaven.

And as wonderful as the biblical descriptions are, they're only a glimmer of the reality to be experienced.

The best we can do is describe the greatest things we can imagine—but even that falls short. Streets made of gold. A mansion prepared just for us. A crystal sea beautiful to the eyes. A place where we'll enjoy all that is good, all that is right. A place where we'll enjoy the absence of evil, sin, and death. We'll all be able to sing there in perfect harmony—what a worship service that will be!

But there's a good chance that when we first glimpse heaven, it will be like nothing we could have imagined. As Paul said, "Eye has not seen, nor ear heard, nor have entered into the heart of man the things which God has prepared for those who love Him" (1 Corinthians 2:9).

I (Mel) recall taking my children to Disneyland. We talked it up big for six months before the trip. We went online to see pictures and read about all the rides. We talked about it at bedtime, imagining what it would be like. But I'll never forget the looks on their faces as we walked through the gates. Their eyes were wide open, looking up, down, across, and at everything that moved. I turned to my son and said, "Is this what you thought it would be like?" All he could say was, "Better, Dad. Much better!"

I have no doubt we'll also be exclaiming, "Much better!" as we first compare the sight of heaven with all that we've imagined.

HOPE OF GLORY

We cannot talk about experiencing the resurrection without talking about the hope we have in Christ—the hope of a better place after our physical bodies pass away.

In Christ, we have a hope that the world doesn't have. Paul spoke of "the mystery which has been hidden from ages and from generations" and that God has made known "this mystery…which is Christ in you, the hope of glory" (Colossians 1:26–27). The greatest mystery in the world is that God desires the resurrected Christ to dwell in the hearts of those who believe and to be their "hope of glory."

Biblical hope is not like the world's hope. To the world, hope is wishful thinking. But when our hope is in God, we have confident expectation that He'll do everything He has promised. Hope in God has no doubt; it is not questioned. For believers in Christ, hope is reality waiting to be experienced.

Hope in God has no doubt; it is reality waiting to be experienced.

The "glory" Paul refers to when he speaks of our "hope of glory" is the presence, power, and activity of all the fullness of God. "Glory" refers to the manifest presence of God. It's an expression of God's active involvement in the life of His people. Eternal life, therefore, is to live in the presence of God and enjoy His goodness forever!

This is what Paul was saying: "My life has been hard, but that's okay. I have the joy of telling the good news of God. The mystery that has been hidden for ages has now been made clear and is available to all who respond. The mystery of eternal life is Christ in you, the hope of glory. And anyone who has put his or her faith in Jesus Christ has, at the same time, received the hope of glory."

A GLIMPSE OF THE ETERNAL

So what is this *hope* that's found in Christ? What is this place called heaven?

The Bible uses the word *heaven* in a few different ways. It speaks of the "heavens" as a part of the created universe. Specifically, the heavens are everything above the earth (our sky, and the planets and stars that shine their light). David wrote, "The heavens declare the glory of God; and the firmament shows His handiwork" (Psalm 19:1). The beauty we see in the "heavens" God created points us to a heavenly home even more glorious than what we currently enjoy.

The second way the Bible uses the term *heaven* is of greater interest to us. Heaven is also a term to describe the eternal home of God, a realm where He and His angels dwell. Jesus taught us to pray, "Our Father in heaven, hallowed be Your name" (Matthew 6:9). Heaven is a place beyond human experience. It's the source of everything good. It's the object of our hope. It's the future home of those who have put their faith in Christ.

When studying the nature of heaven, the biblical description of it grows through the Bible. The Old Testament actually has only a little to say about what happens to the soul after we die, except that God has a plan for the future. Nor does it speak much about hell, except to talk about "the grave" or "the realm of the dead."

The New Testament, however, lays out a more thorough concept of heaven. Perhaps this is because in His own relationship and presence with the disciples, Jesus gave them such a strong glimpse of what was to come.

So what do we look forward to? What do we hope to find in heaven?

HEAVEN IS FREEDOM

Heaven is a place where all negative things are absent. We'll enjoy freedom from the things that weigh us down here on earth.

It's described this way in the revelation that Jesus gave to John: "God will wipe away every tear from their eyes; there shall be no more death, nor sorrow, nor crying. There shall be no more pain, for the former things have passed away" (Revelation 21:4).

In heaven we'll enjoy freedom from everything that weighs us down here on earth.

According to Jesus, there'll be no more pain in heaven. We all have experienced pain in life, some of it physical and some of it emotional. We know those who struggle with chronic pain and who can find relief only through heavy medications that leave them numb and confused. Their pain limits them and saps their strength, constantly reminding them that all is not well in their physical life. But according to the Bible, we'll leave these old bodies behind and receive a new resurrection body free from pain and sickness.

In heaven there'll be an absence of tears—there's no more crying. We know the agony we feel when our hearts are broken, when we see our children struggling, when a loved one passes away, or a myriad of other things that seem to rob our joy and fill us with sorrow. In heaven, the Lord will wipe away every tear, and there'll be no more crying.

There will also be no more death in heaven. No more saying good-bye to those who are dear. The resurrection has conquered death, and eternity has the victory. So many families have sat at the bedside of a loved one dying in the hospital and have felt the pain and agony of the approaching separation. They've felt the unparalleled sorrow of deciding to "pull the plug" and let their loved one slip away. But in heaven, that will never happen again.

In heaven, there'll be no more sin. What a thought! It's a place with no more temptation to do what is wrong. We look forward to a place where sin and its destructive force has no hold on our lives.

I (Mel) will never forget working in a psychiatric hospital while in seminary. I listened to a sixteen-year-old boy say that if he hadn't been arrested and put in the locked facility, he would've been dead in six months. His drug habits were such that he couldn't stop, even though he knew his sinful lifestyle would certainly kill him. As a pastor, I've seen and heard many horrific evils like this that are destroying lives daily. But in heaven, there is no more sin.

HEAVEN IS FULFILLMENT

Heaven, however, is not just the absence of things which cause us sorrow. It's also the presence of everything that brings true joy.

Heaven is so great that the apostle Paul could hardly wait to get there. "For to me, to live is Christ, and to die is gain." Paul spoke of "having a desire to depart and be *with Christ*," which would be "far better" than anything on earth (Philippians 1:21, 23). What a hope!

> *Heaven is the presence of everything that brings true joy.*

Paul's concept of eternity is rooted in the hope of resurrection—of being in the presence of the resurrected Lord Jesus. There was absolutely no fear of death in Paul's heart. He knew heaven was waiting to fill his life full with the goodness of God.

In heaven, we'll experience perfect love—and there's nothing a person wants more. There's no more loneliness in heaven, but only pure love beyond description. We'll be enveloped in God's loving arms, and we'll remain in His loving embrace for eternity:

> Who shall separate us from the love of Christ?... I am persuaded that neither death nor life, nor angels nor principalities nor powers, nor things present nor things to come, nor height nor depth, nor any other created thing, shall be able to separate us from the love of God which is in Christ Jesus our Lord. (Romans 8:35, 38–39)

Heaven is also a place of fellowship. We'll enjoy the blessing of friends old and new. Jesus said, "Many will come from east and west, and sit down with Abraham, Isaac, and Jacob in the kingdom of heaven" (Matthew 8:11). Think of all the heroes of the faith we'll get to know there. Think of walking up to Samson and saying, "Give me a flex." Or sitting down with Moses and asking, "What were you thinking when the Red Sea opened up?" Or asking Joshua, "What was the look on the enemies' faces when you came up in battle?" There are many things to ask Peter. "Tell me about the angel freeing you from prison!" and "How did it feel to defy gravity and walk on water with Jesus?"

Beyond the many biblical men and women who have captured our imagination, there are also our own personal heroes. Perhaps a grandfather who established a foundation of faith for your family. Or a child of yours who slipped into eternity before you. You can chase down all the old relatives you've heard your parents talk about but never actually met.

We can look forward to an eternity with friends and family who we never seem to have enough time with on earth. *Fellowship*—there'll be a lot of it going on in that place we call heaven.

Heaven also is described as a place of rest. In Revelation, a voice from heaven cries out, "Blessed are the dead who die in the Lord from now on." And God's Spirit responds, "Yes...that they may rest from their labors, and their works follow them" (14:13). All our hard work and earthly service to God will end in eternal

All the things you've done for the Lord over your lifetime will be rewarded in heaven.

rest. Are you tired? Are you weary? All the things you've done for the Lord over your lifetime will be rewarded in heaven. There's rest that awaits us there.

When we get to heaven, all will be made known, because it's a place of full knowledge. "For now we see in a mirror, dimly, but then face to face. Now I know in part, but then I shall know just as I also am known" (1 Corinthians 13:12). Is there anything you don't know? You will! Anything that doesn't make sense about this old world? You can ask the One who created it. You can know all things with perfect knowledge when you get to heaven, where our minds are opened up to the wisdom of God.

Heaven is a place of great reward. There's vindication for the Christian. He or she has chosen well and lived right and now is vindicated before all people. "For the Son of Man will come in the glory of His Father with His angels, and then He will reward each according to his works" (Matthew 16:27). Our motivation for serving the Lord is not the prize, but there *is* a prize—a crown of glory and much, much more.

We'll be rewarded for everything we do for the Lord. Therefore Jesus commanded us, "Do not lay up for yourselves treasures on earth, where moth and rust destroy and where thieves break in and steal; but lay up for yourselves treasures in heaven" (Matthew 6:19–20). Our minds can't get around what those treasures might be. You can think of the greatest thing in the world—yet you aren't even close to imagining heaven's riches.

Above all, heaven is a place where we'll see the Lord face to face. "Blessed are the pure in heart, for they shall *see God*" (Matthew 5:8). The apostle John tells us this about the Lord: "We know that when He is revealed, we shall be like Him, for *we shall see Him as He is*" (1 John 3:2). Oh, to enjoy the presence of the Lord! What can we say? It's one thing to look into the heavens and see His handiwork. It's another to look straight into His face and see His love.

WISHFUL THINKING

We could go on and on about the hope of glory and the place we call heaven. But hear this carefully: not everyone will see heaven.

That's a hard reality, but true nonetheless. There are some whose hope *is* wishful thinking, for they don't know the risen Lord.

If there's any message that comes clear in the Bible, it's the simple fact that those who choose to have a relationship with God through Jesus Christ will spend eternity with Him in heaven, while those who choose not to have a relationship with God through Jesus Christ will be separated from Him in hell.

Jesus made this point abundantly clear: "Most assuredly, I say to you, unless one is born again, he *cannot* see the kingdom of God" (John 3:3). He also stated, "I am the way, the truth, and the life. *No one* comes to the Father except through Me" (14:6).

Paul reinforced this teaching that Jesus is absolutely the only way to eternal life with the Father: "For there is one God and *one Mediator* between God and men, the Man Christ Jesus" (1 Timothy 2:5).

A clear division of humanity into two parts will be revealed at Judgment Day. There will be those who have done the Father's will and those who were led by their own desires. Jesus spoke about the dividing line between them: "Not everyone who says to me, 'Lord, Lord,' shall enter the kingdom of heaven, but he who *does the will of My Father in heaven*" (Matthew 7:21).

The Bible is not short on terrifying words to describe the destination of those who remain in sin and miss out on eternal life. Jesus warned, "If your eye causes you to sin, pluck it out. It is better for you to enter the kingdom of God with one eye, rather than having two eyes, to be cast into *hell fire—where 'their worm does not die, and the fire is not quenched'*" (Mark 9:47–48).

He also said,

> The Son of Man will send out His angels, and they will gather out of His kingdom all things that offend, and those who practice lawlessness, and will cast them into *the furnace of fire. There will be wailing and gnashing of teeth.* Then the righteous will shine forth as the sun in the kingdom of their Father. He who has ears to hear, let him hear! (Matthew 13:41–43)

It's only those who have been forgiven of their sin through Jesus Christ, and who have been born again by the Spirit of God, who will see heaven. What amazes me is that those who aren't Christians struggle with that concept—although this was their choice! It seems odd that those who never come to the house of God on earth would want to live with Him forever in heaven. People curse the name of God on earth, yet feel as though they have the right to join with the saints and worship Him around the throne for all time.

It seems odd that those who never come to God's house on earth would want to live with Him forever in heaven.

People who deliberately choose sin on earth will not enter the holy place where there is no sin. People who have rejected Christ on earth will not enjoy His presence in heaven.

Jesus said,

> For God did not send His Son into the world to con-
> demn the world, but that the world through Him might
> be saved. He who believes in Him is not condemned; but
> he who does not believe is condemned already, because he
> has not believed in the name of the only begotten Son of
> God. (John 3:17–18)

Charles Spurgeon had a way with words. He explained in one of his sermons how it is that we can know where our souls will be in eternity:

> You may know very readily. Where does your soul delight to
> be now? Your delight prophesies your destiny. What you've
> chosen here shall be your portion hereafter. If you loved sin,
> you shall be steeped up to the throat in it, and it shall burn
> around you like a liquid fire. But if your delights have to do
> with your God, you shall dwell with Him for eternity.

Spurgeon is right—our time on earth sets our direction for eternity.

HOPE FOR ALL

Apart from Jesus Christ, the fear of death is universal. But resurrection hope of eternal life in heaven is for anyone who would receive Christ. This eternal life is not exclusive; it is open to all. For as many as would call upon the name of the Lord will be saved.

The Easter message proclaims that the resurrected Lord Jesus rescues His followers from the horror of death. We'll not only survive death, but be raised from it. We'll be given new bodies like Jesus' resurrection body, bodies with new and undreamed-of powers.

And our hope of heaven is based not upon our abilities, but on Christ's work on the cross and the Father's work in the resur-

This hope is in Christ, not in us.

rection. That's why this hope is for all; it's not about us. *Christ* is the One who gives us access to heaven. This hope is *in Christ,* not in us. He rose from the dead to lead us through life, and that brings great hope. The all-knowing, all-powerful God of the universe is walking with us. How could we not have hope for the future when God is leading us? How could we not know joy in life, for God Himself is walking with us?

You can always tell a person who knows the Lord. There's a confident expectancy and a joyful hope that will never be disappointed!

NEVER THE SAME AGAIN

For if we have been united together in the likeness of
His death, certainly we also shall be in the likeness of
His resurrection.

—ROMANS 6:5

What an encouraging word—*resurrection*. It's a word full of hope, a word that inspires and brings courage to those who know Jesus Christ. He's the risen Lord, in whom all authority has been given in heaven and on earth. And those who are in Christ are in a good place.

As you've been enlightened about the nature of the resurrection, we pray that you're challenged to live according to the new life you received the moment you put your faith in Christ. That relationship is the most important part of your life. If Jesus had not been raised from the dead, this relationship would not be possible. But because He has been raised, this relationship is the heart of who we are. If you don't have Him, you don't have anything.

Knowing that He did not want you to perish but has a significant purpose for your life, don't be satisfied with anything less. Jesus died for your sin, rose again, and offers abundant life. It's not something He did, but something He's doing right now in your life. So go back and ask the Holy Spirit to examine your life and see if you're experiencing the resurrection as God intended.

Are you truly *living*, in the eternal sense of the word? Do you know the forgiveness of sin through Jesus Christ, and are you living free from its grip on your life? Death is separation from God; life is abiding in His presence. Can you say you're in His presence right now, without anything hindering that relationship? If not, then bring the power of the resurrection to bear upon your life by asking Christ to come and cleanse you of all sin. In prayer, repent of your sin and ask Him to bring you into the presence of almighty God.

Are you experiencing an uncommon life? Are you living in such a way that people see Christ in you, doing that which you could not do on your own? If not, why not? Don't act like a mere mortal; live the life God has given you as a child of God. You partake in the divine nature and have the capacity for so much more than the world around you. Don't limit

Are you experiencing an uncommon life?

yourself by your abilities, but allow the resurrected Christ to live through you in power. Die to self, and allow Christ complete lordship of your life. This life is not about what you can do for God, but what He can do through you. In prayer, tell the Lord that your life is His to use. You want your life to bring glory to Him.

Are you experiencing resurrection peace? You don't have to live with guilt and shame, but can experience a soul at peace with God. Every time Satan reminds you of your past, just remind him of his future. Christ has won the victory, and you're free! If your past seems to be haunting you, holding you back from moving forward, stop and pray. Ask the resurrected Lord to fill you with His peace. Ask Him to confirm in your spirit that you are completely forgiven and in right standing with God.

Are you full of the joy of the Lord? Jesus expressly stated on many occasions that His resurrection brings great joy. Even in the midst of trials, you can have joy that cannot be taken away. It means that circumstances don't control your heart, but the Spirit of the Lord does. So if you've slipped into depression and have lost the joy of your salvation, stop and pray. Ask the Lord to do what He promised—to fill you with His joy. Ask Him to cause His joy to burst forth into visible expression, that others might be drawn to Christ, who is alive in you.

Are you living with resurrection power? The power that

raised Jesus from the dead is the exact same power that's at work in your life. Those areas of your life that have been dead are now

You now have the capacity to know God in His fullness.

alive. Your spirit has been awakened, and you now have the capacity to know God in His fullness. That power is at work to bring abundant life.

So if you sense there must be more to the Christian life than you're experiencing…there probably is. And it's to be found only in a relationship to Christ. Ask Him to open your spiritual eyes to see all that He has prepared for you. Linger in His presence as long as it takes to become fully aware of His life in your life.

Are you living under the authority of Christ? Is your life worthy of the gospel? The life you've received is to be shared with those around you who are still dead in trespasses and sins. Christ has given you the keys of the kingdom of heaven. He has entrusted you with the greatest power on earth—the power of the gospel. Share it freely, live it fully, and share the power of the resurrection with all people. We'll be held accountable for what we've done with the gospel, so ask the Lord to use your life to bring others into the kingdom. Don't watch from a distance, but get in the game. Pray for the Lord to give you an opportunity to be a part of His great plan of salvation.

Are you standing strong, confident in your walk with God

and grounded in Christ? Or are you easily shaken by circumstances? Stability, faithfulness, and confidence are marks of one who's walking with Christ. Ask God to show you what you have trusted in for life's stability. It could be your job, your family, your health, or your talents. None of those can compare to trusting wholeheartedly in Christ. If you're aware of things that have replaced Christ as the foundation of your life, ask Him to forgive you. Ask Him to rebuild your life.

Are you living in the hope of your salvation, or are you afraid of death? There should be no fear of eternity in the heart of a believer, but confident expectation that everything God has promised is *yes* in Christ. When that's true—when eternity is secured in your heart—the petty things in life cannot weigh you down. The little things are irrelevant compared to an eternal reward in heaven that's everlasting in nature.

Are you experiencing the resurrection of Jesus Christ in everyday life? If you've truly met Him, life cannot be the same again. If you're a believer, He is in you. The divine Son of God fills you with His presence.

Our great desire is that you personally live in the power of the resurrection. No more excuses…just clear evidence that you have been with Jesus.

We pray that the world would look at the church today…and marvel.

"O Death, where is your sting?
O Hades, where is your victory?"
The sting of death is sin,
and the strength of sin is the law.
But thanks be to God, who gives us the victory
through our Lord Jesus Christ.
Therefore, my beloved brethren,
be steadfast, immovable,
always abounding in the work of the Lord,
knowing that your labor is not in vain
in the Lord.

—1 Corinthians 15:55–58

DARE TO GO THERE

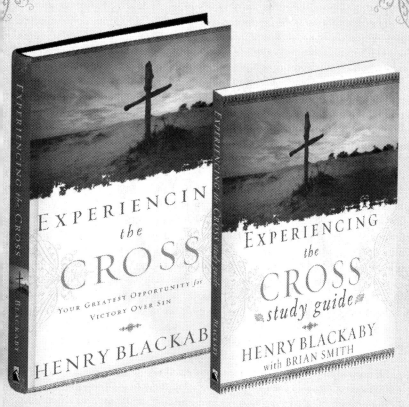

Henry Blackaby leads you on an exploration through the deeper dimensions of the cross, ensuring that the further you go, the more you will: Deal radically and completely with sin, embrace true and lasting union with Christ, and experience the fullness and reality of His victory in your life. Will you yield to God's provision in His cross? Will you receive the power and presence of Jesus Christ? Will you dare to experience the cross? **Study Guide Also Available.**

WALK HIS STEPS, PRAY HIS WAY

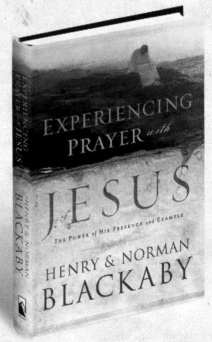

It's not an activity. Nor a chore. Prayer is a way of life. Here's how you can move beyond rituals and discover new intimacy with Jesus. Henry and Norman Blackaby's thorough study of Jesus' prayer life reveals astounding truths about God's intent for prayer. By the time you turn the last page of this 2006 National Day of Prayer book, your old notions will be replaced by the reality of Jesus' example. You'll experience the power of heaven and earth being joined together as the King of all creation lays His heart over yours. Your will becomes aligned with His. Discover freedom from methods and formulas, the beauty of a gentle step-by-step reformation process, and let God unfold His mighty purposes for you.

Experience the Resurrection in Your Daily Life!

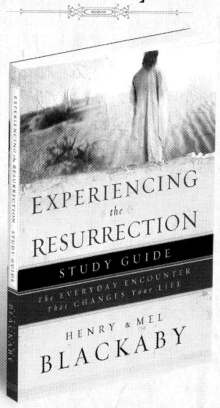

With practical notes, advice, and questions for reflection, the *Experiencing the Resurrection Study Guide* encourages readers to apply the joy of the resurrection to their daily lives. Each chapter of the core book is explored in a one-week format with suggested life change objectives for each day.

Printed in the United States
by Baker & Taylor Publisher Services